Sting in the Tail

By the same author

Lost Heritage
Understanding the Bible through Eastern Eyes
Fighting Poverty through Enterprise
The Jubilee Gospel

Sting in the Tail

The parables as Oriental stories

Dr Kim Tan

Anchor Recordings Ltd

72 The Street, Kennington,
Ashford, Kent TN24 9HS.

First published in 1998 by Bethel Books, Normandy Cottage, Pirbright Road, Normandy, Surrey GU3 2HU

This edition published in 2013 by Anchor Recordings Ltd. 72 The Street, Kennington, Ashford, Kent TN24 9HS.

A catalogue record for this book is available from the British Library.

ISBN: 978-1-909886-17-9

CONTENTS

To my father, who still speaks to me in parables,
to Ben and James, who love stories and telling tales(!)
and to Sally, for her loyal support.

PREFACE

My love affair with the parables of Jesus started a number of years ago and for the past few years they have been the principal subject of my studies. Like many books, this one started life as a preaching series and I am grateful for the opportunity of those weekly meetings at Fox's Barn, where my thoughts were first committed into words. My sincere thanks to the group of men who were the first to benefit from my studies.

I am indebted to the many authors who have written on this subject. Readers will see that I have been heavily dependent on their insights and observations. My initial interest was stimulated by Jeremias' Parables of Jesus, which has remained a classic to this day. However my greatest debt is to Kenneth Bailey's masterly book, 'Poet and Peasant and Through Peasant Eyes.' This is a superb exposition of the parables within the milieu of the Middle Eastern environment. If after reading this book readers will go on to read Dr Bailey's book, "the real thing", this author would have achieved part of his objective.

The sub-title of this book deserves an explanation. The word Oriental is used loosely to refer to the Eastern civilisation, including the Middle East. Regrettably the parables, along with the Bible, has largely been viewed and understood down the centuries through Western eyes. From Augustine onwards, our faith has been hijacked and changed from a Middle Eastern faith to a Greek/Western one. This pivotal change brought an alien world-view and philosophical thinking to our faith resulting in distortions which have continued to this day. This book seeks to understand the parables in the setting of the Middle Eastern culture. They were after all told by Jesus, a Jew, to Jewish listeners in a Jewish culture. There are enormous similarities between the cultures of the Middle East and the Far East and where appropriate I have drawn on these.

I have taken these stories from the gospel of Dr Luke, the gospel for Gentiles. Luke is conscious of the cultural gap between

Jews and Gentiles and has tried to make the story of Jesus understandable to his Gentile reader(s). He does not assume that his reader is familiar with the Jewish background and is therefore more descriptive in the telling of Jesus' stories. He has also chosen stories that he feels are particularly relevant to his Gentile readers. We owe it to Luke for recording the stories of the Good Samaritan, the Lost Sons, the Two Debtors and Zacchaeus, among others. Of the twelve stories included in this book, seven are unique to Luke.

This book is not meant to be a comprehensive study on the parables. That is too big a task. The ones omitted in this volume will, God willing, form the basis of the next. A number of people have assisted with this project including Richard Castro and Stephen Powell. I am indebted to Eddie Tait and Irene Ng for their editorial assistance and to David Pawson for his invaluable comments and encouragement.

Introduction

Western Christians have not been kind to the parables. We have tended to dismiss them as simple stories for children, as rather dull and mundane Bible passages for the Sunday school. Yet Jesus taught his parables to adult listeners!

As I have studied these stories over a number of years, I have become more and more convinced that some of Jesus' most powerful and profound theological statements are contained in his parables. These simple stories reveal truths about the Kingdom, the identity of Jesus, the future and the Church. I have been impressed by what a master storyteller Jesus was. His stories are beautifully crafted and are full of the unexpected. Like scorpions, they have stings in their tails (or tales!).

One of the main reasons we have failed to understand how beautiful the parables are is because we have not understood them as Jesus' listeners did. These stories were told by a Jew to Jewish listeners. They have a Middle Eastern backcloth to them. It is only when we see something of this first century Jewish background that we shall begin to discover the beauty and relevance of these stories. This is the purpose of this book.

In the Middle East and Far East, stories are told to communicate truths, not simply to illustrate them. In the West, we tend to state the truth in an abstract way first. Then a story may be used to illustrate the abstract statement. Preachers invariably use stories to illustrate their sermons in this way. But Jesus told stories which had truths in themselves. That was why, when he was asked, "Who is my neighbour?" Jesus did not respond with a philosophical and theological discussion, but instead told the parable of the Good Samaritan. The answer to the question was contained in the story.

On one occasion when I was in China, I watched a television interview with the mayor of Guandong about the open door policy China now had with the West. The reporter asked if he was concerned that the new policy had opened the door for all the decadent practices of the West to come into his country.

Instead of answering the question directly, the mayor just said, "When you have an old house which has been closed for a long time and you decide to open the doors and windows, you will not only let the light in, but you will also let in the mosquitoes, flies and other insects!" Another classic example of this kind of Oriental story telling in reply to questions comes from the late Chinese leader, Deng Xiaoping. He was once asked how he would describe the new economic system of China. Since his country was not Communist any more, was it becoming a capitalist one? He responded by saying that it did not really matter what colour a cat was - black, yellow or white - as long as it caught mice!

People in the East tend to think and reply to questions in pictorial rather than abstract form. It is very much the way in which Jesus spoke, especially in telling the parables. And we have to try to work our way into this kind of culture if we really are to understand what Jesus is getting at in the parables.

What are parables?
The word for parable in Greek, *parabole* means "comparison or analogy." In Hebrew the word is *mashal* - "to be like." These words describe parables in broad terms, meaning anything which is pictorial and figurative, whether they are sayings or stories. In the Bible the word parable encompasses four different types of sayings. First of all, there are the **pictorial sayings**. Jesus said, "I am the good shepherd." That is a parable. It is painting a picture in the minds of the listeners. Because the Eastern mind tends to think in picture language rather than in Western abstract terms, their speech is often more colourful.

Then there are **similes** which are also regarded as parables. Jesus said, "Be as wise as serpents and gentle as doves." We have similar sayings in the West; we talk about someone being "as stubborn as a mule" or "as angry as a raging bull." The aim of using such similes is to paint pictures in people's mind and Jesus was a master at this. Parables also include **proverbs**. In the Old Testament there is a whole book called Parables. We know it better as the book of Proverbs. But it is the same word in Hebrew.

Proverbs are parables because they too, paint pictures. But the parables we know best are those constructed as **stories** like the Sower, the Good Samaritan, the Talents and the Lost Coin. These will be the focus of this book.

In addition to these, there are real life incidences in the gospels that explain and fill out the parables. The story of Zacchaeus is the one I have included in this book. In it, Jesus' dealings with the tax collector give us an insight into the parable of the Lost Sheep. He was willing to become defiled by his contact with Zacchaeus in order that a lost sinner could find forgiveness and restoration to God's family. Jesus' entry into Jerusalem riding on a donkey is another incidence that cast light on his parables about the Kingdom of God. Four hundred years before Jesus was born, the prophet Zechariah predicted that a day would come when the King would do exactly that. Kings who went into battle rode white horses. Kings who brought peace rode donkeys. On that occasion Jesus arrived in Jerusalem on a donkey as the Prince of Peace. He was acting out a message of prophetic significance so that people could receive it in a more powerful way and he did all this without having to speak a word.

Features of the Parables

The power of the parables Jesus told lie in his use of features found in good story telling. He uses the kind of **analogy** that makes us sit up and think. He talks, for instance, about new wine in old wineskins. Can the Holy Spirit, which God wants to give to the Church through Jesus, be contained in wineskins which are so old that they cannot be stretched any more?

He utilises **unusual twists and challenges**. A good example is the parable of the Good Samaritan. It is a nice story until it gets to the point where Jesus turns the Samaritan, who is Israel's public enemy number one, into the hero of the story. There is the parable of the Rich Man and Lazarus. If the story had the rich man going to heaven and Lazarus the poor man to hell, his listeners would not have batted an eyelid. But Jesus twists it round so the rich man goes to hell and the poor man to heaven. His stories are full of the unexpected, and it is these that make them memorable and endearing. One should picture Jesus' listeners waiting in suspense for the unexpected punch line to be delivered. In the parables Jesus often invites his listeners to identify with different characters in the stories. In this way the listeners are also expected to be challenged by the message.

While the parables stimulate thought, they often leave people to make their own conclusions. There are a number of parables **without ending**, one being the parable of the Prodigal Son or more accurately, the Lost Sons. Here the eldest son turns up finally at the doorstep of the house where the party is taking place to celebrate his brother's return. But he is undecided about whether to go in or not. In leaving that story without an ending Jesus intends his hearers to go away and ponder on the implications of the story. The parables of Jesus appeal to the intellect through the imagination. They are inspiring as well as provocative, seeking to challenge the listeners into making a response.

Most of Jesus' stories are **true to life**. They come from different walks of it. There is the parable of the Lost Coin, about a woman searching around the house for it; there is the Sower and of the Leaven in the Bread. Jesus was no ivory tower theologian expounding abstract truths. His teachings reveal that he was a very shrewd observer of life - the economic, social, political and religious structures of the day.

In his story telling, Jesus uses **contrast** - the rich man and poor man, the wise and foolish virgins, and the **rule of three**. In the Good Samaritan there are three travellers, in the Banquet there were three excuses. And there is the Talents - three servants given money to trade with. This is classic story telling like the "threesome" of the Englishman, Irishman and the Scotsman.

Jesus also uses **repetition** as seen in the parables of the Talents, the Sower and the Wise and Foolish Builders. Each participant in these stories was doing the same thing but with slight differences. Repetition reinforces the message and with a subtle twist powerfully delivers the punch line.

All the parables describe some aspect of the kingdom of God.

Because twentieth century kings are constitutional monarchs without real power, it is quite difficult to understand the real force of this word "kingdom." The rulers of Jesus' day had absolute power to the extent that some of them took on demi-god status, which made it extremely dangerous to anger them. So when looking at kings and kingdoms in the parables we must understand that Jesus is referring to authoritarian and all-powerful kings, not today's monarchs. Similarly, masters of slaves and servants should not be regarded as benign benevolent employers.

Interpreting the parables
Up until the 19th century, interpretation of the parables was mainly allegorical with many fanciful points. A classic example of how not to interpret parables comes from Augustine of Hippo. In the Good Samaritan he equates "a certain man" with Adam who "left Jerusalem" - the heavenly city of peace from which Adam fell. To him Jericho signified hell. From Jerusalem to Jericho there was a drop of 5,000 feet, hence his explanation of Adam's fall from grace to hell! Thieves represented the devil and his angels and stripping the man's clothes meant stripping Adam of his immortality.

The priest and Levite, according to Augustine, represented the Old Testament priesthood and prophetic ministry which were now useless. The Samaritan was the Lord Jesus himself; the binding of wounds is the restraint of sin; oil is the comfort of good hope and wine the exhortation to work with a fervent spirit! The beast, said Augustine, was the flesh in which Jesus came and the man being put on the beast represented belief in the incarnation. The inn was the Church where travellers are refreshed, though it did not matter to Augustine that the Church had not started when Jesus told the parable! Augustine said the "morrow" was the day after the resurrection; the two denarii was either the two precepts of love or the two sacraments, the innkeeper was the apostle Paul, although Paul was not around when Jesus told the story! The promise to pay any extra expense was either his counsel of celibacy or the fact that he worked with his hands.

The danger of this kind of allegorical interpretation is that you can make the Scriptures mean anything you want. As a witty adaptation of a line from a hymn puts it: "Wonderful things in the Bible I see; some put there by you, some put there by me!"

Much more serious than Augustine's interpretation of the Good Samaritan is his exegesis of the parable of the banquet. A rich man invites his friends to eat dinner with him. In Jesus' story, the three invited guests made excuses not to come, so the rich man told his servants to go into the highways and byways and compel those they met to come to the feast. Failing to understand or totally ignoring Middle Eastern custom of the day, Augustine used this parable to justify conversion by force. At its worst this led to the killing of hundreds of thousands of people throughout history. Did Jesus really mean that people should be forced to become Christians by compulsion, putting a gun to their heads or a knife to their throats? Is that the gospel? Surely not. Augustine has done the Church a great disservice with that particular line of interpretation.

A look at the cultural background would have shown that it was considered rude to accept an invitation without a show of reluctance - hence the banquet holder's instructions to "compel" people to come. In Oriental culture it is regarded as impolite to be too eager at accepting an invitation. Furthermore, these outcasts living in the highways and byways would have felt embarrassed to accept the invitation as they would not be suitably dressed and would feel undeserving of the honour. Hence the need to persuade or compel them.

We do not have to look as far back as Augustine for poor exegesis of the parables. The Prodigal Son has been identified as a Christian and the eldest son as a Jew by some more recent commentators. The parable of the Sower has also been used in the Church as a racist argument against Jews -- the thorns being interpreted as the Jewish religious leaders, whereas the good soil was the Church. These anti-Semitic interpretations ignore the context, background and cultural manners of the Middle East and should be treated as dangerous and irresponsible.

Such allegorical exegesis came under attack around 1900,

largely by a German scholar called Julicher. He believed that all parables should have only one point. Jeremias and other major scholars, including the Englishman, C.H. Dodd, adopted a similar approach. To allegorise or not to allegorise was the question at that time. On the whole, most scholars now accept this principle and allegorisation has largely been discredited.

But the pendulum has swung too far. To say that the parables have only one point is too restrictive. Jesus was such a great storyteller and crafted them in such a way that they have many points like the many sides of a diamond. Middle Eastern story telling is subtle, full of nuances and listeners are asked to "listen" for these subtleties. Like a machine gun, spraying bullets at everyone, Jesus' stories contain something for every listener. Whilst answering the question "Who is my neighbour?" in the Good Samaritan, he takes a swipe at the temple system and the inadequacies of the Law. He usually spoke to a mixed audience and different parts of his stories will be particularly relevant to each group.

Understanding the parables

There are at least four different levels to understanding the parables of Jesus:

1. **Aesthetic**. At the simplest level the parables can be viewed as beautiful, charming stories, the kind we can tell children again and again.

2. **Ethics**. At another level Jesus' parables can be appreciated for their ethical content. They tell us how we should live and behave, how we should relate to each other.

3. **Theological**. This is getting deeper, right to the heart of the parables. Here they reveal something of the secrets and mysteries of the Kingdom, things we do not yet completely understand.

4. **Christological**. Here we gain understanding of the person of Jesus himself. Not all parables contain this revelation of Christ, but some of them have this hidden statement about who Jesus is.

Not all parables have all these four elements. Some have just one or two. We need to go into the parables to unpack them and look for these features. Whilst enjoying the parables for their beauty and ethics, they were not the primary intention that Jesus had when he crafted these stories. His intention was to teach deep truths about the nature of the King and his Kingdom. Behind his ethical demands are theological assertions. We need to see the theological nature and thrusts of these stories. Parables may be simple stories, but they are not simplistic. They are packed with lessons, points, messages and different aspects of truth. Jesus invites us to come to grips with these. Some of the most profound theology was taught by Jesus through his parables. A number of things about the mysteries of the Kingdom are so difficult to understand in abstract terms that they can only be communicated in picture language. There is the picture of the king who had gone away to receive the kingdom and then returns. How else could Jesus explain his going away and his Second Coming? It is vivid, powerful and memorable.

Jesus invites his listeners to identify with one of the characters in the stories, to step into their shoes and to make a personal response. His stories are clearly aimed at different groups of listeners. It may be for the crowds, the disciples, the religious leaders or a bit for each of them. His messages are such that each group knows when he is talking about them just as on one occasion when "the priests and Pharisees knew he was talking about them" (Mt. 21). Whilst many of Jesus' criticisms and sayings were directed against the religious leaders, they were not meant to be taken in an anti-Semitic way. The religious leaders of his day had an oral tradition that had turned their faith into a legalistic observance of the Law. This resulted in an arrogant and complacent attitude among them with a deep contempt of those who do not or cannot keep the Law. But religious bigots are not confined to Jews alone. They exist in every religious faith. Jesus is highly critical of the hypocrisy and arrogance of independent, self-righteous people in every culture. It just so happened that the ones within his earshot were the Jewish leaders of his day. Readers should therefore see the attacks levelled by Jesus on the Pharisees as directed at all self-righteous religious people everywhere.

Context

An important element in understanding the parables is the context - cultural, social and literary. There is a cultural gap between modern-day Western society and first century Israel. So before we apply the message of the parables to our situations today we need to understand their message, as they were originally spoken by Jesus to his listeners. We need to go back into the past to make the stories real before we can make them relevant for the present. What did our Lord mean then? How did his listeners understand the parables? We need to learn something of the cultural and political background, about the economic, social and domestic life in the Israel of those far-off days.

There is also an Old Testament background to many of the parables. Jesus' listeners would connect the story of the Vineyard (Mark 12:1-12) with Isaiah chapter 5, where Israel is compared to a vineyard. Israel is also pictured as a flock with God as the Shepherd. We need to be attentive to these Old Testament "echoes" and allusions because Jesus and his listeners would have been familiar with them.

Knowing the context of the gospel in which we find the parable will also help us to understand them. There is a difference between similar parables in Matthew and Luke because the former gospel was written to Jewish believers whereas Luke's was aimed at a recent Gentile convert. Each author may give the same story a different emphasis to draw out different messages for their audiences. For example, the Lost Sheep is identified by Luke as an unbeliever whereas in Matthew it is the little child who is so precious that God is "not willing that any of these little ones should be lost." Again in the Parable of the Banquet, the emphasis in Luke's gospel is on the outcasts and Gentiles coming to the feast, whereas in Matthew the story is directed at the religious leaders coming to the wedding banquet dressed in their old clothes. Guests who have not come prepared for the feast were thrown out. The different emphases in the gospels are, therefore, due to the authors addressing the parables to different groups of people.

The gospel writers often give us clues about the setting of the parables. The parable of the Good Samaritan was told in answer to questions from a lawyer about loving one's neighbour. The parable of the Talents was given as Jesus was approaching Jerusalem during the last few days of His life on earth. The historical settings help us in our understanding of the stories, giving us a sense of the urgency and poignancy of a situation.

Style

All literature fall into certain genre (fiction, biography, history and so on) and each has its own style of writing. The parables, too, have their own literary forms. These stories told by Jesus were passed on by word of mouth until they were written down by the gospel writers. Down the centuries one of the main forms the Jews used for memorising is known as parallelism. This simply means that there is a repetition or an echoing of the same ideas throughout the story in some form of discernible pattern so that it is easy to remember. A simple example is in the Psalms:

"Bless the Lord O my soul

And all that is within me bless his holy name."

The second line is a repetition of the first using different words. There is also "*inverse parallelism or chiasm*" as scholars have found in the parable of the Lost Coin.

The woman had ten coins:

A   One was <u>lost</u>

B   She searches until she <u>finds</u> it

C   There is joy in the community

B'   because she has <u>found</u>

A'   that which was <u>lost</u>

Remembered and recorded by Luke, they are like the keys on a piano. As you move up and down the scales, you play the same notes except in reverse order when you are coming down. It may also be compared to climbing a mountain. You pass over layers of rocks until you get to the top. As you descend, you pass over the same rocks but in reverse order. The style helps the message of the parable to stick in the memory. The parables may also have been remembered and recorded in scenes like a series of snapshots making up the whole story. Understanding something of the styles of these stories will add to our appreciation of the beauty and genius of these parables.

Our approach

The approach we shall take in this study will incorporate all the various aspects we have discussed so far. We will set the parables in their historical context and allow the cultural and social background to make them come alive for us. We will divide the stories into scenes as one would when making a movie. We will tell the stories through these scenes. Finally we will have a summary of the themes of each parable and seek to make them relevant to us for today.

1

THE TWO DEBTORS
Luke 7:36-50

It was a gathering they had all been looking forward to. They knew the food would be good. The added bonus was that the young controversial rabbi who had preached at their synagogue that morning had also been invited. That meant they could really blow apart his strange ideas about God, religion and the Law. They rubbed their hands with glee when they heard he had arrived. Then a woman came in and spoiled the party...

This is a marvellous story within a story. It is a bit like one of Shakespeare's plays called Hamlet. In it there is a scene where Hamlet brings a troupe of actors into court to act out a murder scene similar to the way Hamlet's father was murdered by the man who succeeded him to the throne. The audience watches the acting and the reaction of the guilty king at the same time. Two stories are going on simultaneously. That is exactly what happens here. We shall see that the parable of the Two Debtors is set in the story of the Two Sinners - the "sinful" woman and the self-righteous Pharisee.

The drama opens with Simon the Pharisee inviting Jesus to dine with him. Presumably Jesus had preached in his synagogue. After they arrive at Simon's home the third "character" in this story is introduced: "a woman who had lived a sinful life in that town."

Scene 1: The Pharisee's invitation
It was customary to invite the visiting speaker home to Sabbath lunch. Not only would the meat be carved up, but his sermon too! The Pharisees were very particular about contact with anything unclean - especially unclean food and people. That, in their book, defiled them. Jesus is fully aware of this when he accepts the

invitation. This has an important bearing on the story, because an unclean woman is going to join the dinner party and create an embarrassing scene before the self-righteous Pharisees.

It was a regular event: rabbis lounging around at a meal having theological discussions. Jesus comes into Simon's house and reclines at the table with the rest. Reclining around a table is a sign of wealth or standing in the community. Ordinary people did not have tables, but simply lolled around a patch of floor in the centre of the room where the dishes were placed.

One commentator on a typical Middle Eastern scene of Jesus' day said it was: "a public affair. The gateway of the court and door stand open. A long, low table or more often, merely the great wooden dishes, are placed along the centre of the room and low couches on either side on which the guests, placed in order of rank, recline, leaning on their left elbow, with their feet turned away from the table. Everyone on coming in takes off his sandals or slippers and leaves them at the door... Servants stand behind the couches and placing a wide, shallow basin on the ground, pour water over it on the feet of the guests. To omit this courtesy would be to imply that the visitor was one of inferior rank ... Behind the servants the loungers of the village crowd in, nor are they thought obtrusive in so doing." (Tristram).

Lounging around banquets, celebrations, feasts and debates was really the entertainment of the village and town in those days. The doors were always open and everyone was free to walk in uninvited. There was no such thing as a private dinner party. It was open to the community to participate in the background hoping to catch snippets of conversation, if not some of the specially prepared food. This is still the scene in many Oriental villages today.

That is how the woman came to be at the dinner party which Jesus had been invited to. She went and stood behind him at his feet. One commentator, Ibn al-Salibi, puts it well: "She stands behind him because she is ashamed to approach his face for he knows her sins, and because of the respect she shows to his person."

Feet are considered unclean and offensive in Oriental society. The Old Testament tells us that the biggest insult one could show to a defeated foe was to order them to lie down and then put one's feet on their heads -- to "make your enemies a footstool" (Ps. 110:1; cf 60:8; 108:9). In Malaysian society it is rude to show the soles of your feet to the host and fellow guests when sitting down. This is in contrast to Western society, where feet are regarded as important parts of the body and care is taken of them. The Middle Eastern society of Jesus' day looked on feet as unclean and needed washing when coming into a house.

Yet Jesus' feet were not washed when he came into Simon's house. In fact, he did not receive any of the formal greetings expected in that society. This underlined the low view Simon the Pharisee had of Jesus. He did not offer Jesus any water for his feet neither was he greeted with a kiss, which was also customary. Failing to kiss a guest on either cheek as he entered was a real sign of contempt or at least a heavy hint of the host's higher social position. Jesus was invited to the party as a rabbi because Jews loved to pay their respects to rabbis. A pious Jew would always want to greet a rabbi, yet Jesus was not accorded an honour he was entitled to. Simon's failings were glaring. They were part of a calculated insult to Jesus.

Simon also fails to anoint him with oil. This is probably the least offensive of Simon's neglect to his guest. Although it was a very common practice, it was not obligatory. But washing of the feet and the kiss of greeting were. Another observer of Middle East customs and social habits said:

"The studied insolence of Simon to his Guest raises the question of why he had invited Jesus to his house. When a guest is invited to anyone's house, he expects to be offered the ordinary amenities of hospitality. When the guest is a rabbi, the duty of offering hospitality, in its very best manner, is well recognised. But Simon invited Jesus to his house and proceeded to violate every rule of hospitality ... In the East when a person is invited to one's house it is usual to receive him with a kiss. In the case of a rabbi, all the male members of the family wait at the entrance to the house and kiss his hands. In the house, the first thing that is attended to is the washing of the guest's feet. None of these civilities were offered to the Master." (Levison).

So Simon invites Jesus to his home, having acknowledged him as a rabbi, but proceeds to insult him by neglecting all the formal greetings expected. He was a very judgmental host. Even in the West certain etiquette and formal greetings are expected when welcoming guests. You say "Hello," shake hands, hug or kiss, help them to take their coats off, offer them a seat and so on.

To ignore or neglect any of these is insulting to the guests and may even give out the message that they are inferior. This is precisely what Simon is doing here. When the guest is a guest of honour, somebody important, the insult is doubly serious.

Scene 2: The woman's action

The second character in the story now takes centre stage - "a woman who had lived a sinful life in that town." All the Arabic translations of the Scriptures present her as actively engaged as a "sinner" in the locality. She was a prostitute plying her trade in the locality. Simon the Pharisee knew full well who she was. She was an outcast in the community by virtue of her past.

According to the narrative, this woman does four dramatic things for Jesus. She washes his feet, wipes them, kisses them and then anoints them. She had found out that Jesus had been invited to Simon's house for dinner. Word about such happenings gets around small communities such as this one, very quickly. She either entered with Jesus or before him, because Jesus said that from the time he entered the Pharisee's home she "has not stopped kissing my feet" (vs. 45). The incident makes more sense when we accept that the woman was already there when Jesus arrived, as suggested by Bailey. She was present to witness the lack of greetings and Simon's insulting treatment of Jesus when he entered the house.

It is clear that she had come to anoint Jesus' feet, because she brought the small alabaster jar of expensive perfume. But she had not planned to wash his feet because she had nothing with which to wash and dry them. In the end she resorted to using her hair. This woman had heard Jesus' message of forgiveness of sins and responded to God's overwhelming love. It had stirred a deep desire to show some kind of grateful response, a sign of someone who has truly had their sins forgiven.

She arrives at the house with an expensive vial of perfume, described by one commentator as being "worn by women around the neck and hung below the breast ... used both to sweeten the breath and perfume the person" (Edersheim). It is easy enough to see how important this perfume was to a prostitute. Now, however, she did not need it for herself any more because she had given up her trade, so she decided to pour the perfume on Jesus' feet. It was a beautiful thing that this repentant woman set out to do for Jesus. It would be unthinkable for her to anoint his head because a sinful woman could not do this to a rabbi. That would be disrespectful

When she gets to Simon's house she is horrified at seeing the way Jesus was insulted. She sees him staying silent despite this treatment. He is expected to protest, but he absorbs the insults and hostility. The woman saw that Jesus did not even receive a kiss of greeting. She could not kiss him herself because that would have been very easily misunderstood, for everyone knew who she was. What can she do? Suddenly it dawned on her: She can kiss his feet! So ignoring, or forgetting, that she is in the midst of men hostile towards her, she rushes to Jesus. When she gets to him she breaks down in tears. But instead of wiping them away with her hand, she lets them run down her cheeks to literally bathe the Master's feet with them. As she weeps over our Lord's feet she realises that she has no towel to wipe them with. It was no use asking Simon for one! So she lets her hair down and uses it to dry Jesus' feet. After that she kisses his feet again and again before pouring out her precious perfume on them.

This is a very moving, tender scene, but it is also a very embarrassing one to those hard, religious men watching all this. The woman was offering her devotion to the Lord. In those four dramatic acts she tries to compensate for the insults and neglect of Simon the Pharisee. In letting down her hair she does something very bold and which would be misunderstood. For this was a very intimate act. A woman could only let her hair down in the presence of her husband. To do so in front of another man was grounds for divorce according to Talmudic teaching. So there would have been gasps from Simon and his dinner guests when this woman did just that. The whole room would have been electrified by this woman's "impropriety".

The Talmudic instructions about stoning a woman caught in adultery or of an immoral woman, throw more light on the boldness of this woman: "The priest seizes her garments. It does not matter if they are rent or torn open until he uncovers her bosom and loosens her hair. If her bosom was beautiful he did not expose it and if her hair was comely he did not loosen it." It was as shameful for a woman to let her hair down as it was to expose her breasts. These instructions were given to priests to prevent them having immoral thoughts when called upon to exercise judgement on an immoral woman. In an Oriental culture, the act of this immoral woman loosening her hair in the presence of these respectable male dinner guests must therefore have been profoundly shocking.

Washing Jesus' feet and wiping them with her hair may have been spontaneous acts. But anointing them with her expensive perfume was the very thing this woman came prepared to do (vs. 37). It was the custom that noblemen who visited the homes of kings and priests should have their heads anointed with oil. This woman, clearly, could not anoint Jesus' head, because that would have been presumptuous. But she could anoint his feet. In doing this she not only gave honour to the Master, but showed her humility as a servant as well. "She was extending to him the kind of tribute ordinarily shown only to a nobleman in the house of a king" (Bailey). It is one of many beautiful little touches which add to the impact of the story.

The kissing of Jesus' feet was not only compensation for what Simon refused to do, but also a very public gesture of humility and devotion. In the rabbinic writings, Jeremias tells the wonderful story of a man who was accused of murder and his lawyer skilfully proved him innocent. The freed man fell at his lawyer's feet and kissed his feet again and again in sheer gratitude for clearing his name and saving his life.

In contrast to Simon, this woman tries to make up for the deficiencies and hostilities suffered by Jesus. And, amazingly all this takes place without any spoken word which would have been out of place in the presence of such costly and tender expressions of devotion and gratitude.

Scene 3: A wrong judgement

Simon's astonished reaction to the woman's actions was to say to himself, "If this man were a prophet, he would know who is touching him and what kind of woman she is ... a sinner" (vs. 39). Some manuscripts translate the beginning of this verse as "If this were **the** prophet ..." Simon's dinner invitation to Jesus was to see if he was a prophet or even **the** prophet promised in Deuteronomy, one who is like Moses sent by God in the last days.

The Pharisee mutters a protest to himself that the mere presence of the woman is offensive and defiling even without acting the way she did. He and his friends feel contaminated because she is a sinner both morally and ceremonially. It is a haughty judgement. He also makes a wrong judgement about the young rabbi: "Surely he cannot be a prophet because he is too blind to see that the woman is a prostitute!" He and his fellow Pharisees would consider Jesus to be defiled by this woman's action. All Simon saw was an immoral woman causing a scene with her weeping, letting down her hair and shocking everyone with her bold acts of devotion and gratitude to Jesus.

The guests' hostility was initially directed at the woman, but as she washes Jesus' feet with her tears and begins to wipe them with her hair the hostility switches to Jesus for not refusing her attention.

Traditional Oriental culture forbids touching between the sexes in public, even between husbands and wives. To this day, in some Oriental cultures, wives have to walk a certain distance behind their husbands - they certainly do not walk side by side holding hands. Public cuddles between parents and children were not common until recently. So it was even more startling for the judgmental Pharisee and his dinner guests to see the woman touching Jesus and our Lord allowing her to do so.

The word "touching" in Greek means to light or kindle a fire. In Scripture it is used in the context of sexual intercourse (Gen. 20:6; Prov. 6:29; 1 Cor. 7:1). Obviously this is not the intention here, but Simon's use of the word has clear sexual overtones. Simon is thinking that it is very improper for Jesus to allow himself to be touched like this and, if he was a prophet he would know who the woman was and would refuse her attention. This is what would have been expected of him. Had Jesus wanted to win the approval of the Pharisees rather than demonstrate the mercy of God to this woman, he would have acceded. It was a complete misjudgement of the whole scene by Simon. Jesus knows who this woman is (vs. 47). He also knows her actions are not the impure caresses of an immoral woman, but the outpouring of costly love from a repentant sinner. In Simon's eyes she was a sinner and would always be one. He does not believe that she has genuinely repented.

The interesting thing is that Simon knew who the woman was. It does not imply immorality on his part. But who knows? In a village or small town immoral women are known by everyone. Jesus could have come into contact with her previously when she received the message of forgiveness. Here he is receiving the gratitude of a forgiven sinner. This is really the story of the "prodigal daughter" who has come home to her community, a lost sheep returning to the fold. Jesus is glad to welcome her, but the religious authorities would not do so under any circumstances.

Simon and his guests are unconvinced about the woman's repentance. Worse still, she is a woman. This was a male-dominated society where women were treated as second class citizens. They were classed together with juveniles, as *persona non grata*. They could not give testimony in court as a witness. This is all the more striking when we remember that the first witnesses of Jesus' resurrection were women! There was a group of Pharisees called the "bruised and bleeding Pharisees" because they believed that they should not even look at women in public, even if she was a sister, a mother or a wife. Every time they saw a woman they closed their eyes and walked into walls! Hence the name.

What would Jesus do? He beckons Simon over to him: "I have a word to say to you." The phrase is used across the Middle East as an introduction to some blunt talking the listener may not want to hear. Simon indirectly acknowledges his failure as a host by addressing Jesus as "Teacher." If he is worthy of being called "Rabbi", he is surely also worthy of the honour due to the title that Simon had withheld from him. Why did the Pharisee not welcome him, lining up the male members of his household by the entrance to attend to what was customary of good hospitality? In the Garden of Gethsemane, Judas identified Jesus for the soldiers by kissing him on his hands. But Simon did not kiss him or wash his feet or anoint him with oil.

Scene 4: The Parable

How is Jesus to persuade Simon the Pharisee and his other dinner guests that this woman has been truly forgiven and needs to be restored to the community? They have rejected her, doubting the authenticity of her forgiveness despite this great act towards our Lord. Jesus does what he always does in such situations: he tells a story. In the West we would have started a philosophical discussion on morality, marriage and other related subjects.

The parable is a very simple one about money lending. One debtor owed 50 denarii, the other 500. Both had their debts cancelled. The first amount was the equivalent of two months' wages, the latter two years' wages. Money lending was very common and widespread. It was forbidden in the Old Testament Law, but the Jews had a great ability to get around the Law and ran loan-sharking businesses charging high interest rates. It gives us an insight into the socio-economic conditions of the day. Debt is a terrible thing and increases the spiral into poverty. This is why the Old Testament had two tremendous humanitarian programmes with the Sabbath and Jubilee years during which debts were to be cancelled. The former took place every seventh year and the latter every fiftieth year.

The problem with debt is that a person keeps on digging a bigger and bigger hole for himself. People in Third World countries know that very well, for most of their income goes to meeting debts. Unless they can somehow get themselves out of the hole, they will always be in debt.

Throughout the Scriptures the word "debt" is the same as "sin." So when Jesus prayed: "Forgive us our sins," it was exactly the same as "Forgive us our debts." Jesus skilfully plays with words here.

In this story Jesus states a number of things:

1. Both were debtors. He does not specify gender, but assumes that both debtors were men because he is going to apply it to this woman. It is very deliberate story telling.
2. Both were unable to repay their debts. Both were on the same level. Both had needs and could not help themselves. They both needed help.
3. The same grace is extended to both. The moneylender freely forgives them and offers them grace. The Greek word for "forgive" means "to cancel debt." So "Forgive us our sins" can equally mean "Cancel our debts." In the Lord's Prayer, Jesus is teaching us to pray: "Cancel our debts against you because we have cancelled the debts of others also."
4. The only difference between the debtors is the amount. Jesus asks Simon, "Which of them will love him more" for cancelling the debts? Simon replies, "I suppose ..." Simon realises he is caught in a trap and lamely answers correctly. The logic of the parable is inescapable: love is the response to undeserved and unexpected grace and mercy. He who is forgiven much will love much. That is still true today.

Scene 5: The woman's action replayed

The story could have finished there. Jesus could have left Simon and his dinner guests to work out the implications of the parable, which were clear enough. But he does not stop there. Having established the principle of forgiveness, Jesus now applies it to the woman.

Jesus now says two things which are absolutely outrageous in an Oriental context. Firstly, he praises the woman in the presence of male company. In such a male dominated society, to have a woman praised and men put down is simply not done. But Jesus very boldly comments favourably on the attention and respect shown by this woman in contrast to the Pharisee's neglect. This praising of the woman over a "righteous" Pharisee was shocking. It would be taken as an affront to Simon's high standing in society. As if that was not enough, Jesus then proceeds to complain about the hospitality he has received. Guests in an Oriental society do not complain about the hospitality, but are expected to show appreciation for any they receive, no matter how meagre it is. Not to do so would be considered rude and insulting. A guest is expected to say how honoured he is to be shown such hospitality, that he is not worthy to be received in this sort of way. The host is supposed to respond by downplaying his kindness with something like: "No, no, no, I'm sorry we haven't set a more lavish banquet for you because you're really far more honoured than what has been set before you." It is all part and parcel of the culture that you do not insult your hosts. By complaining Jesus therefore did something regarded as impolite.

It is important to notice how he makes this complaint about the hospitality: "... he turned towards the woman and said to Simon ..." (vs. 44). The speech is obviously addressed to Simon, but is spoken facing the woman. Had he spoken facing Simon it would have been considered as rude. But we see our Lord's gentleness in skilfully putting across some pretty tough things to get Simon to see what had happened with this woman. At the same time Jesus is expressing gratitude to a woman in need of encouragement. She has just performed a very unusual public act of devotion. She is feeling the hostilities of the dinner guests. Has she done the right thing or has she embarrassed herself as well as Jesus? Jesus now encourages her by commending her actions.

Jesus says to Simon, "Do you see this woman?" Simon has seen nothing else since she came on to the scene! Then he says, "I came into your house ..." meaning, "I became your guest, but you did not extend to me the traditional hospitality and greetings. But this woman whom you despise has compensated generously for your failure."

Jesus mentions Simon's three failures in his hospitality:

1. "You did not give me any water for my feet."

Jesus was not complaining that Simon had not offered to wash his feet. That would have been presumptuous and implied that Simon should have acted as a servant. But, if the Pharisee had given him water, Jesus would have been happy to wash his own feet. By contrast the woman had washed his feet with her tears. What a contrast it was too - Simon who offered no water, which was cheap and readily available; the woman who offered her tears, which were costly, produced out of pain and suffering.

2. "You did not give me a kiss."

Equals kiss each other on the cheeks. The disciples kissed the rabbi's hand, so did the servant greeting his master and the son greeting his parents. Contrary to popular belief, Judas greeted Jesus in the Garden of Gethsemane by kissing Jesus' hand, not his cheek, to identify him to the soldiers because there was a disciple-rabbi relationship.

When the Prodigal son returns, the father runs and throws himself around the young man's neck and kisses him to prevent him from falling to the ground to kiss the father's hands or feet. The woman kissed Jesus' feet again and again. The father kissed the Prodigal again and again. These lovely gestures are windows that enable us to see something of God's heart.

Simon should have greeted Jesus as a rabbi. All the members of his household should have been standing at the door to kiss Jesus' hand as he entered. Sensitively Jesus does not mention that his hand was not kissed - only that he did not receive a kiss. By omitting to mention the hand he avoided another insult to Simon. So there is another contrast: Simon, no kiss; this woman, kept on kissing "from the time I entered."

3. "You did not put oil on my head."

Olive oil was commonly used for anointing the head to refresh guests. Then, as now, it was plentiful and cheap. By contrast, this woman had anointed Jesus' feet with very expensive perfume. So Jesus was saying to Simon, "You didn't even give me cheap olive oil, but look at what this woman has lavished on me."

Jesus tells his host, "Therefore, I tell you, her many sins have been forgiven ..." He is not forgiving her sins there and then because they have already been forgiven. He makes this statement in the perfect past tense - her sins have been forgiven. He is just confirming what has already happened in her life. Her actions are a reflection that she has received forgiveness - "for or because she loved much." The Pharisees had condemned her saying, "She's a sinner". But she had come into Simon's house to show her gratitude and devotion, to express her love because her sins had been forgiven. She is no longer immoral. She is not trying to earn her forgiveness by these acts of love, but her heart is so overflowing that she needed to demonstrate her gratitude.

Jesus has another dig at Simon by saying, "... he who has been forgiven little loves little." He is not implying that his host is so righteous that he has very little sin, but that he has little awareness of his many sins. Therefore he has been forgiven little and could only love little. Jesus identifies Simon's failures as a host - failures which are indicative of deeper things such as pride, arrogance, a judgmental spirit and of sexism.

This parable therefore actually presents the listener with two sinners. The first is the woman who has been accepted for her many sins and responds by showing much love. The second is Simon the Pharisee who has no awareness of his many sins, feels little need for grace and shows little love, if any.

The rebuke to Simon is stunning. He is the great unrepentant sinner, not the woman. The prophet has not only read the woman's heart, but this Pharisee's as well. The judgemental one has now become the accused. The drama began with Jesus under scrutiny. Now the tables are turned and it is Simon who is exposed. He loves little because he has been forgiven little. In this we see something of Jesus' identity revealed. Simon's test of a prophet was his ability to know a person's innermost thoughts. Jesus passes this test with flying colours. Not only does he know what is going on in the woman's heart, but deep in other hearts, too. The unique Son of God is revealing himself as a prophet sent by the heavenly Father to proclaim forgiveness.

Scene 6: The Pharisee's second protest

Jesus now says two things to the woman: "Your sins are forgiven" and "Your faith has saved you; go in peace." He is confirming what God has already done in her life. He commends her and tells her that her faith has saved her, not her loving deeds. Then he sends her away from those who despised her with peace, shalom, in the knowledge that she has been reconciled with her heavenly Father.

The dinner guests ask themselves a final question, "Who is this who even forgives sins?" It is a question that is left unanswered and the story closes without an ending. We are not told what Simon's response was, nor what conclusions the guests came to about Jesus, whether he was a prophet or the prophet who could forgive sins. Like so many great stories in the gospels, Jesus leaves this one open-ended, expecting his listeners to come to their own conclusions. Certainly Jesus' actions and words would have given every one at the dinner party plenty to talk about for days to come.

THEMES OF THE PARABLE

Let us summarise the major themes of this story:

First, forgiveness is God's free offer. It cannot be earned. Simon was used to earning God's righteousness through fasting, tithing, prayers and other good works. That was what he had been taught. The two debtors were in no position to pay. Forgiveness comes through faith and accepting God's offer. It is undeserved.

Second, the identity of Jesus is revealed. He is seen as God's prophet who knows the thoughts of men and women and who proclaims God's forgiveness. After this incident Jesus' reputation as a friend of sinners would both soar and become even more notorious.

Third, the initial hostility towards the woman was later

transferred to Jesus. Whilst the initial shock was seeing this woman loosening her hair in public and using it to wipe Jesus' feet, the story ends with the dinner guests affronted by Jesus' actions and words. In coming to the defence of this woman, Jesus faced the hostility of the Pharisees in demonstration of costly love.

Fourth, in a man's world, this despised woman is praised as a heroine of faith, repentance and devotion. Jesus was never afraid to use those considered "undesirables" or "outcasts" by society in his teaching. He used an unjust judge, a shady steward and the woman here to teach truths about the kingdom.

Fifth, when we realise how much we have been forgiven we will love much - just like this woman. The one who has few sins boasts of his righteousness and therefore thinks he has no need of forgiveness. This is the danger we can all fall into. We too, can become like Simon the Pharisee and think that we are basically righteous people - upright, honest and trying our best. We have to understand that even good people need repentance. Bad people need to repent of their bad deeds but good people need to repent of their self-righteous good deeds, which God regards as "filthy rags" or literally "women's menstrual cloth or tampons" (Is 64), something you would not want to parade in public.

This woman was willing to humiliate herself publicly to demonstrate her devotion and gratitude to Jesus. We will see the same determination in the father of the Lost Sons and in Zacchaeus - both humiliated themselves publicly as they sought to show their devotion. The greatest thing we need to grasp here in this story is just how deeply God forgives when we repent of our sins. Maybe then we will love as this woman did.

2

THE GOOD SAMARITAN
Luke 10:25-37

The Jericho road. From Jerusalem it dropped five thousand feet in seventeen miles through the bare Judean hillside. A lonely road for the solitary traveller -- and a dangerous one. Even though he could see a fair distance ahead, the robbers were upon him so suddenly that he had no chance of escape. He fought back, but there were too many of them. They rained blows on him until he lost consciousness. When he came round he was not only aware of stabs of pain, but of gentle swaying. Slowly he grasped that he was on a donkey. When his vision cleared a bit more he saw that leading it was the last person he expected to be his rescuer ...

The parable of the Good Samaritan is all about mercy cutting across racial and religious barriers. It is about loving our neighbour even though we may regard him as an enemy. The challenge of this well-known parable is that we can only truly love God by showing this kind of love and compassion.

First Question

The story is divided into two dialogues between Jesus and an expert in the Mosaic Law. The first dialogue begins with a question by the lawyer: "What must I do to inherit eternal life?" This opening question seems on the surface to be rather pointless and self-evident. An expert in the Law of Moses should know the answer: "Keep the law and you will enter into life." The lawyer had been taught that if you observed the Law, you would inherit eternal life. The question was, however, asked "to test" Jesus' attitude towards the Law which was regarded as rather suspect by the Jewish religious leaders. Jesus seemed to flout the law on the Sabbath, on defilement and the temple sacrifices and was by this stage known for his radical and unconventional approach to the Law.

In classical Oriental fashion Jesus answers this question with another question: "How do you read the Law?" In other words, he is saying: "Let me hear your authorities with the exposition" (Bailey). When studying the Law, it was important to be able to quote what earlier rabbis said about it. It was typical for teachers of the Law to say "Rabbi so-and-so said this ... but Rabbi so-and-so said that ..." Jesus is asking the lawyer to quote his authorities. The lawyer instead answers by quoting a combination of two Scriptures, Deuteronomy 6:5 about loving God with all your heart, soul and mind, and Leviticus 19:18 about loving your neighbour as yourself. Jesus is impressed and says that he has answered correctly.

The synthesis of these two Scriptures brilliantly sums up what is at the heart of the Old Testament law. Scholars are divided about whether this summary actually came from Jesus. Mark's gospel seems to indicate that it was unique to Jesus, who had summarised the Law in that manner (Mark 12:28-34). It may well be that such a summary was already known. If so, Jesus endorsed it and made it his own.

There were previous summaries of the Law. One came from Hillel, a rabbi before the time of Jesus who said: "What is hateful to thee, that do not do to another. This is the whole Law; the rest is only explanation." This is a negative saying and Jesus turns it right round to make it positive: "Do to others what you want them to do to you." Interestingly, Rabbi Akiba taught that Leviticus 19:18 about loving your neighbour was the summary of the Law. While these kinds of summary may have been around, it was certainly not part of mainstream Judaism.

In seeking to make an appropriate answer to Jesus' question then, the lawyer may have been aware that Jesus had summarised the Law as loving the Lord your God with all your heart, strength, soul and mind and your neighbour as yourself. The lawyer, having quoted from Leviticus 19:18, now finds Jesus responding by quoting Lev.18:5: "Go and do this and you will live."

Second Question
Jesus tells this legal expert that he has the right theology - now he has to go and live it out: "Do this and you will live." The word

"do" is in the continuous sense, meaning "Keep on doing this and you will keep on living." Jesus agrees that complete obedience to the Law is the way to be right with God. But can you love the Lord your God with all your heart and all your mind and your neighbour as yourself **all the time**? This bright lawyer realised this was impossible, so attempting to "justify himself" he starts a second dialogue and asks: "Who is my neighbour?"

There are always hot potatoes in religion. One of them among the Jews of Jesus' time was the "neighbour" issue. The Jews' understood "neighbour" to mean a friend, relative or possibly a fellow Jew. That was the answer the lawyer was expecting Jesus to give, because the rabbis and Pharisees all agree that the word "neighbour" in Leviticus 19:18 mentions "one of your own people." It does not include non-Jews and foreigners - "We don't have to love them!"

In classical Oriental style, Jesus answers this second question by telling this great parable, which we will now study in seven scenes:

Scene 1: The wounded man
The seventeen-mile journey from Jerusalem to Jericho was an extremely dangerous one. Jesus is deliberately vague about the man who was attacked and robbed. Nothing is known about him, but his audience would have assumed he was a Jew. Because of the hostility between Jews and Samaritans, the devout Jew would travel on the other side of the Jordan in order to avoid Samaria. The beating he received showed that he had struggled with his attackers, otherwise they would just have stolen from him rather than leaving him stripped naked and half-dead.

The rabbis have very precise definitions about various stages of death. There is a category where a person is just about to die. The category before that is the condition of the man in this story. He is half-dead, which means "next to death." He is unconscious and near death. So he cannot cry for help.

In the Middle East a person's accent and clothing identified one's place of origin. But there was no way of telling who this man was, where he came from or what his religion was. These details have been skilfully omitted by Jesus to create the tension that is at the heart of this story. If it had been obvious that he was a very important person and a Jew, the first traveller to come across him lying there would have unhesitatingly gone to his aid. By hiding the injured man's identity Jesus was deliberately challenging the rigidity of the Law: How do you deal with this situation? How does the Law of Moses teach you to show compassion and humility? The Law says that if he is a Jew you can love him, but what does it say about an unidentifiable person? With minimum words, Jesus has described a scene that is full of tension and drama.

Scene 2: The Priest

The priest is on his way home to the country after a spell of serving God at the temple in Jerusalem - the highest possible duty for a priest. So he is feeling righteous and religious. He would almost certainly have been riding on a donkey, not walking, for priests belonged to the upper class. They were the elite and had tremendous influence in Jewish society. No one with any kind of status in the Middle East walked such journeys in desert country. Only the poor did - and Jesus did!

Also, if the priest had been walking he would not have been able to help the robbers' victim, apart from giving him a bit of first aid. It is vitally important to assume he was not on foot, otherwise the story loses its impact. The priest had to be in exactly the same position as the Samaritan to offer help. Jesus' listeners would have understood it this way.

The priest is in a dilemma. He is bound by the Law and the commandments, yet he is wrestling with a sense of duty. He has two basic fears as he sees the badly injured man. He is, understandably, afraid of being ambushed, for the robbers might still be around. But he is also afraid of being defiled.

He does not know who the unconscious man is, or the state of his injuries. Looking across the road at the bloodstained figure, it crossed his mind that he could even be dead. If he was dead, the priest could become ceremoniously unclean - doubly so if the man was a Gentile. Of the five sources of defilement in the written Law, contact with a corpse was top of the list. The oral Law listed four more sources - and contact with a non-Jew topped this list. The Law even forbade the priest to come within four cubits (6.4 ft) of a dead person, let alone touch the body.

The consequences of defilement were dire. The priest served in the temple, administered various services and functions and collected, distributed and ate tithes with members of his family. Defilement for him would mean that the tithe of tithe, called a wave offering, which was given by the Levites for consumption by the priest and his household, could not be eaten. He would be banned from officiating at services and forbidden to wear his phylacteries.

It would also be costly and time-consuming to become ritually clean again. First he would have to present himself at the temple in Jerusalem. Next he would have to buy a red heifer and offer it as a sacrifice. Finally he would have to stand with the unclean during the temple sacrifice and when the gong was sounded during the offering of the incense be shamed publicly for becoming unclean.

In any case, it would be humiliating to have to return to the temple so soon after his period of service there. It would hit his income because the ritual would take a whole week and he would have to tear his clothes.

So what was this priest expected to do? His family, colleagues and even the lawyer listening to this story would all have applauded his decision to pass by on the other side of the road. Jesus is emphasising that this priest is a victim of a rule book, of a rigid ethical and theological system that fails to interpret what is at the heart of the Law: God's mercy. This priest is returning from serving God in the temple, a duty regarded as the height of worship. Jesus deliberately crafts the story to show that whilst the priest may have kept parts of the Law, he has nevertheless broken God's commandment to love one's neighbour.

Scene 3: The Levite

The Levite is also coming home from Jerusalem. Some scholars believe the story assumes that the Levite knows there is a priest ahead of him, because it was possible for the traveller to see a long way ahead on that road. Levites were a lower social class than priests and were not bound by as many regulations. Yet they were still a privileged group, being responsible for the temple liturgy and for policing the building. Levites are descendants of Levi, the third son of Jacob and Leah. Because the tribe was not allotted any land when they entered Canaan, the Levites had no direct means of support. They were to receive a tenth of both the harvest and livestock (Lev. 27:30-33; Num. 18:21 & 24), out of which they had to give a tenth of the tenth to the priests (Lev. 18:26-27).

This Levite could also have become defiled if the injured man was dead. Yet he could have helped him if he had really wanted to. It would not have cost him as much as the priest. He was not in full-time preaching, but in a supportive, deacon-like role. He goes up close to where the man lies but does not help. He has three fears - of being robbed himself, of being defiled and of doing something different to the higher ranking priest: "If he didn't bother to help, why should I?" Why should he risk being berated by the priest?

The Levite passed by because of the bad example of the priest or most probably out of self-interest. Jesus is pointing out that he too, is a victim of the legalistic system.

Scene 4: The Samaritan

After the priest and Levite, Jesus' listeners are expecting to hear that the next man to reach the robbers' victim was a Jewish layman. For priest, Levite and layman, called the "delegation of Israel," served together at the temple. This was the expected "threesome." So imagine their shock when Jesus announces that it was a hated Samaritan who turned up at the scene next! It completely destroyed their anticipation of a nice story about a Jewish layman putting the other two religious types to shame.

The hatred between the Jews and half-caste Samaritans goes back a long way, at least to the return of the southern tribes from exile in Babylon in the sixth and fifth centuries BC. This enmity has its roots in the division of the northern and southern kingdoms after the death of King Solomon, which resulted in two tribes worshipping in Jerusalem while the ten northern tribes did not

The Assyrians conquered the northern kingdom in 722 BC and deported many of the people, replacing them with pagans. They intermarried with the remaining Jews resulting in the Samaritans. Their descendants were not idolaters, but they only acknowledged the Pentateuch (the first five books of Moses) as inspired by God. They worshipped on Mount Gerizim instead of Jerusalem. When Nehemiah sought to rebuild the Temple and the walls around Jerusalem it was the Samaritans who opposed him because their holy place was Mount Gerizim.

Such was the hatred of the Samaritans that the Jews put them on a par of nastiness with the Philistines and Edomites. The Mishnah (the commentary on the Laws of Moses) states: "He that eats the bread of the Samaritan is like one that eats the flesh of swine." So, according to the teaching of the rabbis, receiving kindness from Samaritans was like eating pork, which is of course not kosher. A few years before the Mishnah was written, the Samaritans had defiled the temple by scattering human bones within its courts. So you can imagine the tension rising as Jesus introduces this hated character into the story. The lawyer must wonder what Jesus was going to say next as he builds up to a climax in the story.

It certainly took a lot of courage to have a despised Samaritan in the story, especially as Jesus makes him a morally better man than the two Jewish religious leaders. As one commentator puts it: "Only one who has lived as part of a community with a bitterly hated traditional enemy can fully understand the courage of Jesus in making the despised Samaritan appear morally superior to the religious leadership of the audience. Jesus speaks to one of the audience's deepest hatreds and painfully exposes it" (Bailey). It is like telling this parable to a Protestant audience in Northern Ireland and portraying the Good Samaritan as a Roman Catholic. If Jesus was telling this story to Israelis today, this would be the parable of the "Good Palestinian." It takes real courage to tell such inflammatory stories to a hostile audience.

Another intriguing aspect of the story is that Jesus himself was called a Samaritan (Jn. 8:48), a derogatory term. He is accused in the same breath as being demon-possessed. It is almost as if he is using this parable to turn the table on those who have insulted him.

When the Samaritan came up to the injured man he felt compassion. He was deeply stirred inside and showed mercy - not just a kind, sentimental feeling towards the unconscious man. This word "compassion" is a strong word that comes from the Greek word *spanchnic*, meaning "gut or bowels." It is a word used to describe God's feelings for his people. It is used only three times in Luke's gospel. The first is used of Jesus when he saw the sadness of the widow of Nain whose only son had just died. The second reference is to the Samaritan. The third is used of the father when he sees his prodigal son coming home. In each we are to see the strong feelings of God for his people.

In coming to his aid, the Samaritan was taking some big risks. Like the priest and Levite, he was also in danger of being ambushed. If anything, a Samaritan in Jewish territory was even more of a target than the two religious types who had passed by before him. Sometimes crooks have an odd kind of respect for those in religious garb!

Like the priest and the Levite, he could also be contaminated if the man was dead. This is not often appreciated. The Samaritans were subject to the same laws as the Jews, for the Pentateuch was their Law too. It is vital to our understanding of the Samaritan's subsequent action to realise that he was subject to the same Law as the priest and the Levite who had gone along the road before him.

There was a third risk: retaliation from the man's family and community. The Samaritan could have said to himself, "This man is most probably a Jew. Those two religious Jews down the road have left him to die, so why should I get involved?" But he stops and gets involved.

Scene 5: Binding up the wounds
The Samaritan must first clean and soften the wounds with oil, then disinfect them with wine before bandaging them. But Jesus tells the story the opposite way round: he binds up the wounds

first and then pours on oil and wine. The emphasis is on the binding, and it is a picture of God's healing as he acts to save his people in the Old Testament (Hoses 6). God's first act of healing was to bind up Ephraim's wounds, so a Jew hearing the phrase "binding up the wounds" would immediately picture God binding up the wounds of his people. Oil and wine are standard first aid remedies in the Middle East.

If you had been the lawyer listening to this parable, a thought would probably have crossed your mind: "Wait a minute! The Law says that a Jew cannot receive any acts of mercy or kindness from a Samaritan." It is forbidden to receive oil and wine if they came from a Samaritan. Also, by accepting them the injured man was obliged to pay tithes on them. So the lawyer would have been pleased if Jesus had said in the story that the man had rejected oil and wine from the Samaritan. That is what the wounded man is expected to do.

The Law was such a morass of clauses and sub-clauses that when a Samaritan appears on the scene eager to help there are massive legal problems barring the way. Jesus is emphasising to his hearers that the Law had become so mechanistic that, instead of being a vehicle which expresses God's mercy and compassion, it was actually obstructing it.

Despite all this, the Samaritan shows amazing love for an injured Jew. It is an uncalled-for act of mercy and doubly undeserved because of the hostility between the Jews and Samaritans. And in this act we see Jesus' own offer of unexpected love exemplified.

Scene 6: Journey to the inn

The Samaritan puts the injured man on his donkey and leads it along the road like a servant. Once they get safely to the inn, the story is in a sense complete. But instead of ending it there, Jesus continues with the story in order to add further punches to the parable. He wants us to see the Samaritan staying overnight to take care of the injured Jew as going the second mile, of further self-giving and courage.

Put this part of the parable in another setting. Imagine a Red

Indian finding a robbed and wounded cowboy on the prairie, putting him on his own horse and leading him into a Wild West town rather than to his own tribe. The hostile eyes of everyone in the town would be fixed on the Indian. If the Indian had really feared for his life, he could have left the man at the edge of the town and fled. Instead he goes to the hotel, books a room and carries the wounded cowboy upstairs to nurse him overnight. He then expects to leave town alive in the morning! That is the force of the Samaritan's action.

Hated, despised, with a Jew on his donkey, this Samaritan leads the way into the Jewish town of Jericho under the gaze of its extremely suspicious and antagonistic inhabitants. In the Middle and Far East even today, people are strongly advised not to stop at the scene of an accident, but drive to the nearest police station and report it. If you stop to help, you are assumed to be responsible for the accident and liable to be attacked and even killed. The Jews would have assumed that this Samaritan was responsible for the unconscious Jew's injuries. Having shown courage by stopping to help the injured man, the Samaritan shows more courage in this final act of compassion at the inn.

Scene 7: The promised return

Having made up for the failures of the priest and Levite, the Samaritan now compensates for what the robbers have taken. The wounded man has no money - his attackers took it all. If he cannot pay for his stay at the inn he will be arrested for debt. The Samaritan gives the innkeeper two denarii, asks him to take care of the wounded man and promises to return and repay whatever they have spent on that care. Talk about rubbing salt into the wound!

Innkeepers were pretty unsavoury characters in those days. They had such bad reputations that the word "prostitute" was often used to mean "a woman who keeps an inn." Such an innkeeper would not have been very pleased if this badly injured man could not pay his bill. But this Samaritan, though an unknown stranger, demonstrates love to this needy man he has rescued by paying for everything.

In this act of unbelievable love, compassion and mercy we see the Cross. A debt has been paid. It is Jesus himself who can be seen as the Good Samaritan. We see Jesus going to the aid of a completely helpless, beaten, stripped and half-dead person and binding up his wounds, facing the hostility, suspicion and misunderstanding of the town's people and nursing the man back to health. He pays the price when the man is unable to do so.

There is something intriguing about the Good Samaritan's promise to return and pay what is owed. One day's board during Jesus' time was equivalent to a twelfth of a denarii. The two denarii the Good Samaritan gave to the innkeeper was enough for 24 days' stay - sufficient time for the injured man to recover from his ordeal. The Good Samaritan promised to return after a certain time, in about three weeks. This is really going the second mile.

Another intriguing aspect about this parable is that, in the Middle East of those days the last place to take a wounded man was an inn. The obvious place to take him would be to his own home or a friend's. But if he had been taken to a home, the Samaritan would not have had to pay for him - nor would there be a need to promise to return. By telling the parable the way that he did, Jesus wants his listeners to get the message that this Samaritan paid the debt of this man who was in no position to pay it himself.

As hearers of the story, we would be invited to step into the shoes of one of the characters. It is very clear that we are to identify with the wounded man on the Jericho road. The Lord Jesus himself has found us, picked us up and is going to nurse us back to health and pay our debts because we are in no position to help ourselves. Our salvation is due to his initiative and compassion alone.

Jesus completes the story and faces the lawyer with the all-important question: "Which of these three men was a neighbour?" It was pretty obvious: The Samaritan, of course. Except that the legal expert could not bring himself to name the despised Samaritan. Instead he says: "The one who showed mercy."

To this response Jesus tells him for the second time: "Go and do likewise." The lawyer's problem with this is: "who can love in this way, to consistently be a neighbour of this calibre?" The answer for those listening to this dialogue should have been: "No one." They are meant to conclude that they cannot keep the Law in every situation, but need to throw themselves upon the mercy of God.

Through this parable Jesus is trying to show that the Law cannot save a person. The Law as interpreted by the religious leaders is constrained when it comes to showing mercy. It can actually prevent people from showing mercy and compassion. After showing the limitations of the Law, Jesus introduces an unheard-of dimension of mercy, compassion and divine love. Since the Law cannot save us, our salvation must depend on God's mercy.

The parable of the Good Samaritan is also a commentary on Luke 6:27-36, where Jesus says "Love your enemies ..." He is saying that your enemy is your neighbour! This strikes deep at racial conflicts going back hundreds of years, like that between Catholics and Protestants in Belfast. When there is hostility between two groups of people the "neighbour" is always: "People in our own community," not those from the "other side."

Evangelicals tend to define "enemies" as a individuals. But they could be national or racial enemies, as in the case of the Samaritan. In telling this parable as a commentary on his discourse in Luke 6, Jesus is saying, "Your enemy the Samaritan is your neighbour." In the Sermon on the Mount, Jesus said that there is only one action that demonstrates that we are sons of the heavenly Father, and that is enemy loving. It is only through showing radical love that we will be like our Father. It is the hardest thing that Jesus calls us to imitate him in.

It is easy for us to fight back, to retaliate and maintain the walls of hostility. But the gospel is about tearing down those walls, even among national enemies. It is easier in Britain, but go and tell the Serbs, Bosnians and Croats in the former Yugoslavia or the Hutus and Tutsis in Rwanda that their racial enemy is their neighbour!

THEMES OF THE PARABLE

We can now summarise this wonderful story:

First, the giving and receiving of mercy should transcend

national and racial barriers. Jesus attacks the racism of the Jews - and we are not exempt. He defines loving your neighbour as "enemy-loving". We cannot run away from that. As his disciples, Jesus calls us to this kind of radical and costly love.

Second, the love and worship of God are inseparable from loving our neighbour. The priest, returning from serving in the temple where he has done his religious duties, sees the injured man and does not help. The keeping of the commandments without showing mercy to a neighbour does not fulfil the Law. Also, the oral Law is impotent when it comes to showing mercy. Our faith must be demonstrated in our good works.

Third, the Samaritan shows unexpected grace and mercy - a beautiful picture of Jesus himself. This is a self-revealing parable and Jesus intends us to gain a deeper understanding of him. He had been insultingly called a Samaritan. In identifying with the Samaritan in this story, he is saying that the help we need will come from an unexpected person.

Fourth, the story reveals the supreme courage of the Samaritan. He risked misunderstanding, revenge and racist attack in showing compassion. In paying the wounded man's debt we see the Cross. Unable to help himself, the man had to rely totally on the mercy of the Samaritan. That is us. We are that wounded man on the road and we need the Good Samaritan to rescue us and bring healing.

3

THE FRIEND AT MIDNIGHT
Luke 11:5-13

It was the third or fourth thump on the door that penetrated his brain. His first reaction was to burrow deeper into the blankets. But more knocks followed, louder and louder, forcing him to haul himself out of bed, shouting: "Who is it? What do you want at this time of night?" A familiar voice came faintly from the direction of his doorstep: "I need your help. Someone has just turned up at my place and I've nothing to feed him with. Can you give me some bread and...?"

This is the essence of the intriguing parable Jesus tells after teaching his disciples how to pray. They had been so impressed by their Master's approach to prayer, something men in particular find difficult to do, that they wanted keys on how to go about it effectively. Even though, as Jews, they have been taught at home how to pray, especially by their mothers, they were intrigued by the extra dimensions Jesus brought to his devotions. After teaching them that tremendous prayer we know as the Lord's prayer, Jesus went on to say: "Suppose one of you ..." Or "Imagine ..." This technique grabbed his hearers attention, forcing them to think about which shoes to step into as the story unfolded.

Scene 1: An unusual late arrival
Commentators disagree about whether it was normal to travel at night because of the heat during the day. It may have been normal in countries like Jordan, Syria and Egypt - but certainly not in Israel or the Lebanon. The hills and mountains of Israel, together with the sea breezes meant that temperatures at night were much cooler than in neighbouring nations. The consensus is that it was unusual for anyone to travel by night in Israel. Thieves go around at night. Those who do travel under the cover of darkness do

so for special reasons - especially to avoid detection. Mary and Joseph fled to Egypt at night to save Jesus from being killed by Herod's soldiers.

Arriving at somebody's house at midnight was, therefore, highly unusual. So Jesus would have had his listeners' attention right at the beginning of this story with an urgent need that suddenly emerged out of the darkness. What is the man expected to do when this nocturnal traveller turns up on his doorstep?

Scene 2: An unusual late request

The householder is supposed to entertain this guest. He cannot turn him away because Oriental hospitality is legendary. Because he does not have any food to give the midnight guest, he goes and knocks at his neighbour's door to ask for three loaves of bread. Many commentaries put much emphasis on the figure three and there have been some interesting allegorisations of this down the years. One theory is that three loaves is a meal for one person. That may have been true of the small Syrian loaf, but the ones here are larger.

We need to understand a little about Oriental hospitality to help us appreciate the details here. Anyone who has been in the Middle and Far East knows that the amount of hospitality at meal times can be embarrassingly extravagant, even in poor homes. A guest cannot be given half a loaf of bread, but a whole, fresh one. To serve one that has already been used would be shameful and insulting. Furthermore, you cannot set the bare minimum before your guest. As the host you are expected to set more than is sufficient for your guest. If he can eat one loaf you have to put more than that on the table. Anything less would be considered bad manners. Custom dictates that you must be able to offer second and third helpings. This is why the man in the parable asked for three loaves. In a typical village the women co-operate in the bread-making and everyone always knew who had done some baking recently. So it was easy enough to go and find a neighbour who had freshly-made bread. The host must lay on a meal for his guest whether the latter was hungry or not. Go into any Oriental house and food appears immediately. It is the

Oriental culture. It is the responsibility of the host to do this and show his guest that he can provide for his needs.

Another crucial key to understanding this story is that this guest is not just a guest of the individual householder whose door he has arrived at, but of the village - the community. The picture is of a small village which the traveller has come to. When he departs, the host would say to him: "You have honoured our house" or "You have honoured our village by visiting us." So it is not the individual host's responsibility alone to cater for and entertain this guest. In the West we have lost this sense of communal hospitality with our individualistic lifestyles.

In going to his neighbour to ask for bread, the host is, therefore, asking him to fulfil his duty to the guest of the village. As long as that request was modest and reasonable, refusal was unthinkable. In this case the request was for the humblest part of the meal.

Bread in itself is not the meal. It is the edible equivalent of our knives and forks - the means to eating the meal. A fresh loaf of bread would be set in front of the guest, who would break off a bite-size piece, dip it into a common dish of fish, vegetables or eggs and pop it in his mouth. Then he would break off another and repeat the process. In that way the common dish would not be contaminated. The bread has to be flavoured with something for the meal. The really poor would flavour it with salt. It would be broken and dipped into salt instead of a common dish - hence the phrase, "bread and salt." The equivalent for those in abject poverty in the Far East is rice and soya sauce.

The host in the parable is asking for bread. But the listeners know that he will need other dishes as well. In an Oriental culture it is impolite to ask for everything you need. The host is expected only to ask for the basics. His neighbour is expected to oblige and to offer him other dishes to go with the bread. He is supposed to show generosity beyond what was asked for. Such is the etiquette of the Orientals. The host knows he would have to borrow other dishes to be eaten with the bread. This becomes very clear at the end of the parable when Jesus says the neighbour will get up and give him what he needs. The host has a shopping list and bread is the only one item he can politely ask for! The neighbour will be so concerned that he will get out of bed and show his generosity by giving the host "as much as he needs."

The host is reasonably confident about getting what he needs for several reasons, even though it is a most unsociable hour to call on his neighbour. He is the host, not the guest. So he is not asking anything for himself. He is asking for the most basic of food. He is not asking for something unreasonable. Furthermore, he is going to a neighbour to ask him to honour a guest of the village.

The host tells his neighbour that he has nothing to set before his guest. This is idiomatic, for the host does have food. He has olives, grape-molasses and cheeses. They have been prepared on a yearly basis and stored. All households have those basic foods stored in a loft at the end of the one-room peasant house. But the host does not have everything that he would like for his guest. He will use food from his own store together with what he is able to borrow to lay on as sumptuous a meal as possible.

I have had many great meals on my travels. One I will never forget was when I was preaching at a new church in Sarawak, Malaysia, and was invited home for lunch by one of the leaders. He lived in a longhouse on stilts and we had to climb a long ladder to get into the house. We sat down on matted floors to eat a simple but most carefully prepared meal with this poor family. They had gone to great lengths to show me hospitality and had prepared many dishes. I had not requested it, but it is the way of the Oriental to entertain lavishly. And one feels moved by such expressions of kindness.

That is the kind of picture we have in this parable. The host goes to great lengths to offer hospitality because it is part of the custom. The host is supposed to say to his guest: "What I have set before you is inadequate." The guest, in return, is supposed to compliment the host by saying: "This is a wonderful meal. You should not have gone to such trouble." The host is then supposed to respond: "It is nothing but bread and salt, an ordinary meal. You deserve better." Such then is the way of hospitality in the East.

Scene 3: Unacceptable excuses

With this background in mind, can you imagine anyone turning down this request with excuses like the children being asleep and the door locked? The answer is a clear "No." And that is what Jesus was trying to get his listeners to see.

But the neighbour does make some feeble excuses. He says that the door is bolted on the inside. But it is not a heavy door and it can quickly be unbolted. The text translates literally as, "The children are in bed with me." With only one room in the house there was an area where everyone slept - husband, wife, children. I grew up in that kind of environment, sleeping with my parents and my brother in one room in my early years. Jesus is describing a scene that is real.

These are feeble excuses by the neighbour for not getting up and meeting the legitimate needs of the host. However, Jesus says that even though these excuses are given, the neighbour will still get up. The problem here is that it is a very inconvenient time. It is not that the neighbour is unwilling to help, but he would rather the man at the door come back in the morning. Yet the need is now. So the neighbour has to sacrifice his sleep, get up, light the lamp and search for what his neighbour needs. In this we are to understand that this is a costly request.

Scene 4: The request is met

Jesus says that even though the neighbour will not get up and meet the request out of friendship or obligation, he will do so because of the man's "boldness." Some translations say he will give everything that is needed because of the man's "persistence." But the passage here does not say that it was a triumph for persistence on the part of the host. We will come across that later in the parable of the unjust judge and the widow. There, persistence wins the day. In this story however, we have a different emphasis. The Greek word *anaideia*, translated as "boldness" here, is better translated as "shamelessness" or "the avoidance of shame." The New American Standard Bible margin translates the word as "shamelessness" and Bible scholars now recognise it as the proper translation of the word. The colourful Hebrew and Yiddish word "chutzpah" can mean boldness, audacity or shamelessness and this is what we have here. This passage is therefore better translated: "Yet, to avoid being shamed, the neighbour will get up and meet the needs of the host." In other words, even if the neighbour will not get out of bed because he is a friend, yet because he wants to avoid being shamed he will get up and meet the needs of the host. Otherwise the latter would go round the neighbourhood in the morning and tell everybody that this man could not be bothered to get up in the middle of the night to supply what was needed for a guest of the village. The emphasis here is on the integrity of the neighbour, on his noble and honourable qualities, not on the persistence of the host.

The concept of shame is extremely important in Eastern culture. Much of life is governed by laws, but a lot is governed and controlled by a sense of shame, a fear of losing face and by a sense of honour. Shame needs to be avoided to protect the individual's sense of honour.

Jesus' application

Jesus then goes on to apply the message of his parable. He uses the method known as "going from the light to the heavy!" In other words, if an ordinary neighbour will get up at an inconvenient time to meet the needs of this host, how much more will your heavenly Father respond to your request.

Jesus then makes a telling statement about the father lavishly responding to his children's request. An earthly father would never dream of giving his children a stone when they ask for bread, a snake instead of a fish, or a scorpion instead of an egg. Bread, fish and eggs are ordinary food. Perhaps these are the things that the neighbour had to search around for in the middle of the night. A round stone in the desert does not look too different from a loaf of Middle Eastern bread. One of the things Jesus was tempted to do by Satan in the desert was to turn stones into bread (Mt. 4:4-4; Lk. 4:3-4). A snake - or an eel - does not look very different from a fish and a curled-up scorpion can be mistaken for an egg. Jesus uses these contrasts to emphasise that if this neighbour is willing to get up at great cost to himself to meet the needs of his friend, how much more will our Heavenly Father arise and meet our need when we come to him with a request.

That is why Jesus finishes off this teaching on prayer by saying, "If you then, though you are evil, know how to give good gifts to your children, how much more will your Father in heaven give the Holy Spirit to those who go on asking him!"

THEMES OF THE PARABLE

What are the themes of this simple story?

First, there is an emphasis on the nature of God's help. It is unconditional. His generosity far exceeds what we ask for. The neighbour not only gives the host bread, but whatever else he needs. That is what God is like. He answers us when it is inconvenient. The host knocked at a bad time because he had an emergency on his hands. In these situations Jesus says, "Pray. Ask."

God answers in ways that are costly to him. It cost the neighbour something to meet the needs of the midnight guest. All our prayers are now made possible because of the Cross. I used to think God answered prayer out of his generosity, like signing cheques. It took me a long while to learn that when God hears our requests in prayer, it costs him something.

If you go to a neighbour like the one in the parable, everything is stacked against you. He is asleep, the door is locked, the children cannot be disturbed. But because of his integrity he will get up and give you what you need. God, to an even greater degree, will not deny his integrity. He does not want shame heaped on his name. Because of that he will answer us. He will arise and meet our needs. In the neighbour's action of getting up, getting dressed, putting the lights on and turning his house inside out to come up with all the food the host needed for his guest, we have a marvellous picture of God our heavenly Father giving us far more than we could ever ask for or dream of.

Second, we can have confidence when we pray. If you are confident that such a neighbour will meet your need, how much more can you be assured that when you make your requests to your heavenly Father, he will meet your needs. Even in unusual circumstances, in times of emergency he will answer because of his honourable and noble nature.

It is appropriate that Jesus, having taught the disciples in the Lord's Prayer to pray about daily bread, should go on to tell a parable about a friend who goes on asking for bread. This very simple story contains some very deep truths about the nature of prayer. God is a loving, heavenly Father and we need to learn how to approach him with our requests no matter what the circumstances are or the time of day or night. When he meets our needs, remember that it costs him something. Knowing this may change the way we pray. The Friend at Midnight is one of three parables on prayer, encouraging us to seek, to go on knocking, so that the door will open. More than a parable about persistence in prayer, this story is told by Jesus to encourage us to go on praying because of the kind of God that he is. He is a good God!

4

THE BANQUET
Luke 14:15-24

He had been planning it for months. It was to be the event of the year. No details had been overlooked and nothing had been spared. As the big day drew nearer and nearer the excitement could be felt in the surrounding community. When it arrived everything was going smoothly until his servants rushed in with some terrible news: the guests would not be coming after all. He was aghast, but he quickly ordered his employees to go out and invite a new set of guests. No feast would be quite like this one ...

Jews have something in common with the Chinese - food. With the Chinese it is easy to understand why. Almost anywhere in the world you will come across a Chinese restaurant or takeaway. But Jews? Well, take another look at your Bible. On almost every page we see the Jews having some kind of meal together. The last page of the Bible describes the greatest banquet of all - the Marriage Supper of the Lamb. Meals are important to them. So important that someone has paraphrased Matthew 18:21, "Where two or three Chinese are gathered together there is a restaurant in their midst, but where two or three Jews are gathered together there is a kitchen in their midst!"

This parable took place on a Sabbath day when Jesus was a dinner guest in the house of a prominent Pharisee. Over dinner, Jesus had told them a parable about not taking the highest seat at the dinner table unless invited by the host. He then proceeded to tell them to invite the poor, the crippled the lame and the blind when they have a banquet so that they "will be repaid at the resurrection of the righteous." When one of the dinner guests heard this, he said rather self-righteously to Jesus: "Blessed is the man who will eat at the feast in the kingdom of God." This man had assumed that, as a son of Abraham and because of his own righteousness, he would automatically be there at the great feast in the kingdom of God. Jesus told this parable to sound a warning that this assumption may be dangerously wrong.

He tells the story of a nobleman giving a great banquet, not a Western-style dinner party but a lavish affair typical of Middle Eastern celebrations. It would have been one of the largest events of the village. Such occasions were common in the times of Jesus. But there is something more behind his use of the banquet setting. In the Old Testament there is the concept of a sacred meal with God. In Middle Eastern speech, to "eat bread" means, "to have a meal." This is a symbol of fellowship, of shalom or peace. This would be familiar to the Jews: "You prepare a table before me in the presence of my enemies" (Ps. 23:5). Though surrounded by foes, the psalmist was saying that the Lord as his Shepherd was preparing a meal so that he could still have fellowship with God. For the Jews then, the Banquet is a symbol of salvation. To understand this, we only need to look at passages such as Isaiah 25:6-9. This prophecy gives us a description of God's great banquet at the end times. The food will be the very best - rich, with vintage wine. Isaiah was given a vision of a wonderful event to which all the peoples of the earth would be invited to take part in this lavish banquet with God after death has been destroyed and the veil between time and eternity removed.

The most interesting thing about this vision is that the Gentiles will be there as well as the Jews. From Isaiah onwards the banquet theme was taken up, developed and taught by Jewish rabbis and teachers with one vital omission - the inclusion of the Gentiles. By the time of the New Testament, Jews understood that they were going to be at the banquet as God's chosen people, but they were not expecting any Gentiles to be there.

Those listening to Jesus tell this parable would have understood the banquet in this way, that it was related to the coming of the Messiah and their invitation to attend this event of events was assured. They did not think for one moment that Gentiles and social outcasts such as the blind and crippled would be there.

Scene 1: The rich man throws a lavish party

He invites all the important people to his banquet. An invitation to such an occasion in the West gives us the option of saying "Yes" or "No." But if someone important in the Middle East sends an invitation, there is no such option. It may be an invitation, but it is also a summons. Those invited are to make sure they are there! This is still the case today. In Oriental societies, when an important and influential person makes an invitation, it comes with a summons to be present.

The custom of the time was that invitations would go out in good time before the party as well as on the actual day itself. The second invitation would come just before the food is ready, when slaves would go to those invited and remind them about it. That is still the way things are done in some parts of the Middle East even today. One commentator has pointed out that if a sheikh or emir invites people to a feast, he always sends a servant to call these guests at the proper time, often echoing the words of Luke 14:17: "*Tefuddulu, al'asha hader*" - "Come, for the feast is ready." This invitation has Messianic overtones. The words come to us again in Revelation 22:17 about the marriage feast of the Lamb: "Come, for all is ready."

The first invitation is for the host to know how many people are coming so that he can plan the meal, especially what animal to cook for the main course. If only a small number send in their RSVP he might have a kid prepared. But if many do so, he will order a sheep or calf to be killed. Those invited are expected to accept and, in doing so, are duty-bound to turn up on the day. The second invitation is a reminder that the meal is ready.

Accepting the first invitation obliges the person to eagerly look forward to receiving the second invitation. Failure to accept that second invitation would be a gross insult. Instead of coming to the banquet, the invited guests of this parable unanimously "began to make excuses."

Scene 2: "I've just bought a farm"

The first excuse is that this man has just bought a piece of land

and he must do a survey of it. This is nonsense. No one buys land without surveying it first. Land transaction in the Middle East is a complicated and drawn-out affair. The contract must declare that everything on it is included in the price - trees, fountains, wells and so on. When Abraham bought a field and the cave and trees within it, all the borders were checked before the purchase went ahead. The Oriental listener to this parable would know that this excuse is not merely pretty lame, but an outright lie. The buying of land in the Middle East is a very tedious process. Everything is done on a face-to-face basis. Land is an important part of anyone's inheritance and it is very difficult to sell one's birthright. It can take years to acquire and dispose of land.

The excuse was a severe insult to the banquet host. The event would be held in the evening - and the field could hardly be surveyed in the dark! In any case, time is not important in the Middle East. The survey could wait until tomorrow. In accepting the invitation and then failing to turn up the man was, in effect, saying: "My land is more important to me than my relationship with you."

Scene 3: "I've just bought some animals"

This is another poor excuse. In the Middle East, there are two ways of buying animals such as the oxen mentioned here. One is to go to the city market and inspect those up for sale for strength and health before purchasing. The man's excuse in the parable was that he had already bought the oxen and was going to check them out at home. This involves seeing if they can work together as pairs. The other way of buying such beasts was to go to the owner's field where they were at work. There were no agents in those days; word simply got around that a farmer wanted to sell some of his animals.

This man must have been pretty wealthy to buy five pairs of oxen. Normally one or two pairs were adequate for a small farm. So here he was, saying he wanted "to try them out" - in the evening! How could he judge their performance in the dark? Besides, he could easily wait until the following morning.

His excuse was another big insult. In reality he was saying that his farm animals were more important to him than his relationship with the nobleman.

Scene 4: "I have just got married"
This is quite an innovative excuse and on the surface appears to be the only legitimate one of the three. After all, the Bible provides for a year of release after marriage (Dt. 24:5). But this exemption is from military service, not work. It enables the newly-weds to spend time together, removing the danger of the husband being posted away from home for long periods and the danger of being killed in battle. Attending a banquet for several hours hardly falls into that category! It was just another poor excuse.

This excuse contains a picture of a recent marriage. The wedding was not on the same day as the nobleman's banquet. The community could not cope with two important functions on the same day. In the Middle East men even today are very coy over talking about women in public. It is a male-dominated society and women are kept in the background. But here is this man using his wife as the excuse for not turning up at a banquet! He would have been really laughed at with this excuse. People would have poked fun at this hen-pecked husband who could not even go to the event of the year. Jesus expects his listeners to laugh at this excuse. In effect this guest was saying that his wife was more important to him than his relationship with the banquet host.

Scene 5: The angry master
Understandably, the banquet host is furious at these excuses. The men who made them had previously accepted the invitation but at the last minute had backed out of coming. The key question is, what will the master do? A Middle Eastern nobleman like him would have gone to a lot of trouble to have an animal slaughtered and cooked for the feast along with the rest of the food, and to arrange for the music and dancing. He is expected to feel insulted and get angry. For this man has lost face in the community. If he sends out invitations to rich, influential business and community

leaders and landowners in the area to come to a banquet, their presence at the function is an indication of the respect they have for him. Refusal to come indicates their scorn of him.

The chorus of ridiculous excuses again needs to be understood within the Oriental culture. It is impolite to say an outright "No" to an invitation or a request for help. And so excuses have to be made. Jesus' listeners would have understood the reasons for these outrageous excuses. They were polite but hypocritical ways of saying "No." We see this in the parable of the Friend at Midnight and the feeble excuses of those putting off following Jesus in Luke 9:57-62. But these excuses all add up to a serious insult of the master.

The Oriental master is expected to explode with anger and cancel the banquet. His anger is expected to boil over into some form of revenge. The master does get angry. But to the surprise of his listeners Jesus then says that he reacted in an unexpected way. Summoning his servants, he gives them a most unusual and unexpected task.

Scene 6: Invitation to the outcasts
The servants are sent out a third time with invitations this time to the poor, crippled, lame and the blind. If you were a Jew listening to Jesus telling this story, you would be horrified at the direction this story is taking. What! Surely no self-respecting nobleman holding a plush banquet is going to invite these riff-raff? It is like the down and outs living in cardboard boxes outside London's Waterloo or Charing Cross railway stations being invited to Buckingham Palace. But that is the master's command: Go and invite the rejects within the community to take the place of these important people at the feast. This is scandalous.

Just before he told this parable, Jesus had said that when a banquet is held, the poor, crippled, lame and blind should be the ones invited to it. Shocking - and even more so because of the connotation that this is a Messianic banquet and the Jews had been taught that such outcasts would be excluded from it. But Jesus is saying they will be there, taking the place of those "important" people who refused to come. The Jews taught that the poor were not invited to banquets, the crippled do not get married, the blind do not examine fields and the lame do not test oxen. Such people were excluded from the Messianic banquet. But the master says: "Go and invite them in!"

The master is not indebted in any way to these outcasts. His invitation is an act of pure grace. They do not deserve to be there and he is under no obligation to invite them. They are invited to the Messianic banquet because of the grace of the Master, not because of merit, influence or wealth.

Scene 7: Invite the Gentiles!

The outcasts gladly accept the invitation. The servants go back and report to the master: "They've come, but there's still more room!" Jesus wants us to hear echoes of his own words here: "In my Father's house, there are many rooms" (John 14:2). The "Vacancy" sign is still up.

The master sends out the servants with yet another invitation, this time along the "roads and country lanes" or "highways and byways", which are outside the city, and "make them come in." Scholars generally agree that this invitation is used by Jesus to refer to the Gentiles, who were regarded as outcasts by Jewish religious leaders. Those who travel along the roads and country lanes and sleep under hedges, (which is what "byways" literally means) do not belong to the community.

A Jew travelling to Samaria would not be allowed to spend a night in a Samaritan village, but had to sleep outside the village, under the hedges - as Jesus and his disciples did when they were walking through Samaria. Foreigners also had to sleep in the byways because they were not welcome in Jewish homes. So Jesus is calling for those outside the Jewish community to be invited.

This is doubly shocking to Jewish listeners of the parable. It was bad enough saying the poor, crippled, lame and blind Jews should be invited to the banquet, but these rotten Gentiles as well...! It is unbelievable grace. The fascinating thing is that Jesus is, in effect, restoring the original vision Isaiah had all those years previously of Gentiles being at the Messianic banquet. This is a very important parable for Gentile Christians, for it promises us a place at that great event.

An awful lot has been made of the phrase "make them" or "compel" as justification to use force to persuade people to become Christians. That was the interpretation from Augustine onwards, to put a sword to people's throats and force them to convert to Christianity or die. It is an interpretation that has been responsible for more bloodshed and murder than any other interpretation of Scripture. Hundreds of thousands of people have been murdered because of interpreting the parable in that way.

The key to understanding what "compel" means in this parable lies again in the Middle Eastern culture, where it is considered rude to be over-eager in accepting an invitation. The same is true in the Chinese culture I come from. At meal times in our home, when someone is asked if they want a second helping and they say "No", we ask if this is a Chinese "No" or an English "No". An English "No" means "No. I don't want any more." But a Chinese "No" is a polite "No" which means "No, but I can be persuaded to have some more." It is impolite to say "Yes" too quickly. Furthermore, these outcasts living in the highways and byways would be reluctant to accept such an invitation. They would feel undeserving of the honour, nor would they be dressed for a banquet. Hence the need to persuade or compel them. There is a tone of intensity and urgency about this word.

This is the context of the parable. Those invited will say "No" but will allow themselves to be compelled or persuaded to come to the banquet. Picture yourself getting the final invitation in the parable. You are a foreigner, sleeping under the hedges. You know that the Jews dislike you and treat you as an outcast. Then along comes a Jewish servant who says, "My master is a nobleman who is holding this huge banquet and he's inviting you to it!" You are not likely to say, "Thank you very much, that's very nice. I'll come." Instead you will say, "There's something suspicious here. I don't believe it. Does he really mean it?" Were the down-and-outs of London to receive a dinner invitation from Buckingham

Palace, they too would have to be persuaded or compelled to accept the invitation.

The master knows that that will be the reaction. That is why he specifically instructs his servants: "Make them come. Convince them that it's a genuine invitation." We despised Gentiles who have no place at the banquet, no rights to be there, have received an invitation from the Master. What a glorious thought!

At the end of Luke's gospel, we see Jesus on the road to Emmaus after his resurrection talking to two of his disciples. He really wanted to continue to fellowship with them at Emmaus and to break bread with them. Luke however says that "he acted as if he would go further." The disciples managed in the end to persuade him to stay. Why this play-acting? Again because it was regarded as rude to be over-eager to accept their invitation to eat and stay with them (Luke 24:28).

The parable listeners would now be expected to react: "Why would the master invite such outcasts to this posh banquet?" Those who turned down the invitation, if they were to look at the new guest list, would not want to be there anyway because they would not be seen dead with such characters, especially at a party like this. They were too self-important. "Why does he eat with sinners?" they grumbled about Jesus. It is because of grace.

Jesus gives his listeners a final warning. There will be a judgement on those who have received a formal invitation, especially the Jewish leaders, the Pharisees. The clear threat implied is that if you do not accept the invitation your place will be taken by outcasts and Gentiles. It was very courageous of Jesus to make such a statement in face of the hostility of the Jewish religious leaders. He was, in effect, saying: "None of these men will taste my dinner."

THEMES OF THE PARABLE

We can summarise the themes of this story like this:

First, Jesus claims that the Messianic banquet is being prepared. The guest list is compiled and the invitations are going out. Every guest has to be invited - you cannot gate-crash the party. The invitation is by grace only, not because of wealth, influence or merit. Not because of race or family connections. It is all due to the generosity of the host of the banquet.

Second, those who are invited first, the religious leaders who are presumptuous, will be disappointed and their places taken by those they regard as outcasts and unworthy. There is a clear threat intended here. God's covenant with Abraham will be honoured and the Jews will head up the invitation list. However, Jesus warns that if they refuse his invitation, their privileges will be forfeited and their place offered to those whom they consider unworthy including the Gentiles. In inviting the poor and Gentiles, Jesus is restoring Isaiah's unfulfilled vision.

Third, no excuses for refusing the invitation will be tolerated. Any excuse in the light of the Messianic banquet is insulting to the Master. We are the recipients of the invitation to the Messianic banquet. It is all of grace - unexpected and undeserved. We should come with grateful, humble hearts. There is a warning here that the master does get angry with those who fail to turn up because of feeble excuses.

Matthew's account

Before we leave this story, we need to make some comments about this parable in Matthew's gospel (Mt. 22:1-14). Remember we said that Matthew had Jewish disciples in mind when he wrote it, whereas Luke was written by a Gentile for another Gentile. In Matthew, the story is about a wedding banquet given by a king for his son. This clearly has strong Messianic overtones. The guests refused to come and in fact kill the servants bearing the invitations. The king is furious and sends an army to destroy "those murderers and burned their city." New servants are sent into the streets to invite anyone they can find.

Up until this point in the story, apart from the obvious difference in the settings and the dramatics, the two accounts are reasonably similar in their message. The striking difference comes, however, towards the end of the story. In Matthew's account, the king notices a guest "who was not wearing wedding clothes" and challenges him about his neglect which amounted to an insult to the king. "The man was speechless" - indicating that he could have been better prepared and dressed for the occasion. The king then instructs his servants to bind the guest up and throw him out "into the darkness, where there will be weeping and gnashing of teeth"- words understood by all to describe hell. This dramatic ending needs an explanation.

In Luke's account, the emphasis is on accepting the invitation and coming to the banquet. In writing to a Gentile unbeliever or a recent convert its message is on salvation, on getting to the banquet. Matthew is however writing for people who are already believers, who are already invited to the banquet. The context suggests that he is directing this parable to the chief priests and Pharisees (Mt. 21:45) who assume they have a right to be at the banquet as the descendants of Abraham. Jesus had just spoken to them about the parable of the tenants, and turns to speak "to them again in parables" (Mt. 22:1). They are warned here by Jesus that they risk being rejected because they have not arrived in their "wedding clothes." Something is amiss. They are still wearing their old clothes of self-righteousness. They have neglected to get ready for the banquet thinking they can simply turn up as they are. The message here is that they cannot. They have to get out of their old clothes and put on new ones for the wedding banquet. The invitation is given out of divine grace, but the responsibility to change and get ready is man's.

5

THE LOST SHEEP AND THE LOST COIN
Luke 15:1-10

"One, two, three ... fifty-five ... eighty-eight ..." He had done this so many times without a hitch. Yet he continued slowly and deliberately. "Ninety-nine, one hund..." The shepherd checked himself. What he thought was the last member of his flock by a distant rock was nothing more than a shadow caused by the sunlight. He called his colleague over and told him to take the flock back to the village while he set off further into the wild countryside to search for the missing one ...

Chapter 15 of Luke's gospel contains three parables on the same theme: "being lost and then being found again." The first two are about the lost sheep and the lost coin, which I will deal with here. The rest of the chapter is taken up with what I regard as the greatest parable of all, the Prodigal Son or, more accurately, the Lost Sons. We will examine that story in the next chapter.

Jesus opens with the parable of the Lost Sheep because he is under fire from the Jewish religious leaders, especially the Pharisees, for being friendly with sinners: "This man welcomes sinners, and eats with them." (Lk. 15:2) In Luke's previous chapter Jesus had told a parable in which he defended the rights of sinners and even Gentiles to be invited to God's banquet (Lk. 14).

Now he is going to tell his accusers and others listening that not only do sinners have the right to be restored, but there is joy in the heart of God when the lost are restored to the family. The heart of this parable is joy - the joy of finding the sheep that was lost. This theme of "joy" occurs throughout the gospel of Luke.

It is a parable which begins with a shock for the Pharisees and scribes, because Jesus makes another social outcast, a shepherd, as the hero of his story. In Old Testament times, shepherds were highly regarded by everyone. King David started as a shepherd boy and God was regarded as the Shepherd of Israel. All this changed as owner-shepherds gave way to hired shepherd in New Testament times. Shepherds were now regarded as low life - not just sinners, but men in one of the most despised of professions. They were ceremonially unclean and excluded from the synagogue. The rabbis taught that no one should buy milk or lambs from them because you did not know if they had been stolen. They lead their flock on to other peoples fields and as hired-hands were not exactly courageous at defending their flocks against attacks by wild animals. To use the shepherd imagery, Jesus had to distinguish himself as the *Good* Shepherd. When he opens the parable with "Suppose one of you ..." Jesus identifies these conceited religious types with the shepherds they revile. He is challenging their attitude towards these men to really get them listening to the story.

Scene 1: One of the flock is missing

An average family would have between five and fifteen animals. Three hundred sheep would be considered a large flock, so someone with a hundred would be in the middle income bracket. Some scholars suggest that the flock was not owned by this man alone. They suggest that he was more likely to be a representative of friends, neighbours or extended family in a village who owned the hundred sheep between them. He would have been hired by them to look after the flock of sheep. He would feel the responsibility for the entire clan and any loss is a loss to all of them. According to these scholars, this explains the joy in the whole community when the sheep is finally found. This may not necessarily be the case however. The shepherd in the story calls his neighbour to rejoice with him because, he says, "I have found *my* lost sheep." I believe we are to imagine a relatively wealthy shepherd in this story.

There were two types of shepherd in those days. The peasant shepherd lived in the village and led his flock back to the courtyard of the family home at the end of each day. There was also the nomadic shepherd who left his flock out in the open at night. The shepherd described in this parable is a peasant shepherd.

Two or three shepherds would have looked after a flock of this size. When one sheep is lost and a shepherd goes searching for it, the other shepherds take charge of the rest of the flock. Although Luke says this shepherd left the rest of the sheep "in the open country" to search for the missing one, listeners would have understood that he did not leave them unattended. A shepherd could not look after a flock of a hundred on his own. That was too dangerous. So his fellow shepherds with whom he left the ninety-nine sheep, would lead them back to the village and alert his family that one animal was missing.

The gospel of Thomas, in the Apocrypha, says that the missing sheep was the largest of the flock, implying that it was more valuable. That would distort the meaning of this story. Size is irrelevant. Big or small, this animal was precious - as precious as the other ninety-nine. If anything, looking at the parallel passage in Matthew's gospel, the missing sheep was probably the least important member of the flock (Mt. 18:13-14).

Shepherds normally counted their sheep regularly - at least once a day. They usually do this out on the hillsides. It was a shepherd boy searching for a lost sheep who made the important discovery of the Qumran scrolls. Having forgotten to count the sheep the previous night, he made up for it by counting them twice at the unusual time of eleven o'clock the following morning. Leaving fifty-five sheep with his two companions, his searching brought him to what is now called Qumran Cave Number One and the discovery so precious in terms of archaeology and striking confirmation of the authenticity of so much of the Old Testament scriptures. He went looking for a lost sheep and found other priceless treasure that day!

Scene 2: The searcher finds the missing one

The shepherd searches for the lost sheep "until he finds it". There is a sense of responsibility and determination here. He is the owner and he hopes to bring the sheep back alive. Had he been a hired-hand he would have had to bring the sheep back, dead or alive, because he needs to prove that he has not sold it. God has a similar determination in seeking the lost until he finds them.

The shepherd does find the sheep - alive - probably looking helpless and refusing to budge from the thicket it is in or the rock ledge it has wandered on to. Sheep are notorious for getting into awkward places and becoming stuck. A Middle Eastern shepherd who has searched for lost sheep recalls: "When a sheep has strayed from the flock, it usually lies down helplessly and will not move, stand up or run. Hence there is nothing for the shepherd to do but carry it, and over long distances this can only be done by putting it on his shoulders around his neck."

Here we are to see something of the burden the shepherd faces in carrying the animal. But his first reaction when he finds the lost one after a long, hard search is pure joy. He heaves the animal on to his shoulders and rejoices. The burden on him as he descends the hillside to the village under the weight of this frightened sheep reveals that there is a cost to pay in his search for the lost sheep. It is dangerous being out in the wilderness alone. He is away from the security of his home and the protection of his fellow shepherds and endures dangers and physical discomfort. But he finds the sheep, rejoices and carries it all the way back home.

Through this, Jesus is making it clear that there is a price to be paid in seeking the lost and restoring them to the fold. The shadow of the Cross looms large in this story. In all three parables in Luke chapter 15, Jesus intends us to see that the principal actors paid a price to find the lost. The searching shepherd, the searching woman and the father of the Prodigal during his agonising wait, all reflect what God the Father has to endure to find and bring back the spiritually lost.

Scene 3: Public rejoicing

The weary and hungry shepherd finally arrives home, staggering the last few yards with the lost sheep still on his shoulders. The community welcomes him and rejoices at the safe homecoming of the shepherd and the wayward animal. The shepherd, full of joy, calls the community to rejoice with him. Personal joy is shared with the community because of the strong sense of solidarity in the Middle Eastern culture. The restoration of the lost sheep would therefore be a time for communal rejoicing. This is the pinnacle of the parable.

Middle Eastern thinking is communal, not individualistic. Israel is thought of as one family together. So joy occurs twice in this short parable - first at finding the sheep irrespective of the burden and cost, then throughout the village when the stray is brought back safely to the fold. This joy reflects the greater joy in heaven when a sinner repents because the lost sheep is a picture of the lost sinner. Lost from the community, the sinner is found, restored and can expect communal joy. It is a contrast to the Pharisees' grumbling about Jesus mixing with sinners. These proud religious Jews are the "ninety-nine righteous persons". There is more joy over one sinner who has repented than these religious people who have not done so.

THEMES OF THE PARABLE

We may summarise the parable as follows:

First, there is an emphasis on the joy of the shepherd and the community. Jesus invites everyone, especially the Pharisees and scribes, to rejoice over the conversion of sinners. It is very hard for religious, self-righteous types to rejoice over the repentance and acceptance of those whom they despise - those they have labelled outcasts and worthless.

Second, Jesus wants us to see in this parable that restoration is costly. Jesus defends his welcome to sinners, a welcome which involves restoring them to the community. The shepherd's long search and the burden of carrying the rescued sheep home is costly. The shadow of the Cross is over this parable. In his death, Jesus became the Good Shepherd paying the highest price to save and restore the lost. Nevertheless, it is all of grace and the shepherd's initiative. The lost sheep was unable to help itself. It needed the intervention of the shepherd to rescue it from its predicament.

Third, there is a clear picture of the shepherd's determination. Jesus describes the endless trouble people will take to recover lost property. Success brings deep satisfaction. This is a picture of God's love for the lost. He loved us while we were still sinners. It is unconditional grace, which is why the lost sheep could not have been the largest and most valuable animal of the flock. If it were so, God might not deem us worthy of his search. On the contrary, nothing is spared in seeking and finding every lost person regardless of who and what they are. This parable echoes Ezekiel 34:12, where God is pictured as Shepherd of the flock.

Fourth, Jesus affirms the need for repentance. This applies to sinners as well as those like the Pharisees who think they are righteous. There is a touch of irony in Jesus describing the Pharisees as "righteous persons who do not need to repent". Some rabbinic traditions claim God loves the "perfectly righteous" more than repentant sinners. Rabbi Abba said: "All the prophets prophesied only for sinners; but as for the perfectly righteous (who have never sinned at all) 'the eye hath not seen, O God, beside Thee, what he hath prepared for him that waiteth for Thee." But this is a denial of Scriptures such as Isaiah 53:6, "We all, like sheep, have gone astray ..." Other rabbis such as Ben Sirach did, however, take a different view: "Do not revile a repentant sinner; remember we are all guilty."

Jesus takes a dig at those who think God loves the perfectly righteous more than repentant sinners by saying that even if only one repents he brings more joy than the ninety-nine who think they are righteous and do not need to repent. The New Testament affirms what Jesus is seeking to tell people here, that every one needs to repent. The shepherd in this parable is a picture of Jesus. This adds more insult to the Pharisees because of their low view of shepherds in Israel. However Jesus is drawing on the Messianic picture of the Shepherd in Ezekiel 34 in this parable and his listeners would have been conscious of that.

Matthew's account
As in the parable of the Banquet, there is a slight difference in the emphasis of this story as it is told by Luke and Matthew. Again the key to this lies in the context. In Luke's gospel, this story is

told by Jesus to a mixed company of tax collectors, "sinners", Pharisees and teachers of the law (Lk. 15:1-2). More specifically, Jesus told this story in reply to criticism that he "welcomes sinners and eats with them." Hence the lost sheep in Luke is the unbelieving sinner, the outcast of society. These are the ones regarded as God's rejects by the religious leaders. Jesus' parable teaches us otherwise.

In Matthew's gospel, the context for this story is a discussion by the disciples on "Who is the greatest in the kingdom of heaven?" (Mt. 18:1). Jesus used a visual aid to address this debate. He called a child (*paidion*) and said to the disciples that "whoever humbles himself like this child is the greatest in the kingdom of heaven." Jesus then makes four statements about "these little ones" (*micron*):

1. "Whoever welcomes a child like this in my name welcomes me" (Mt. 18:5)
2. "Anyone who causes one of these little ones who believe in me to sin, it is better for him to have a millstone hung around his neck and to be drowned in the depths of the sea" (Mt. 18:6)
3. "See that you do not look down on one of these little ones." (Mt. 18:10)
4. After telling the parable of the Lost Sheep, he says: "In the same way your Father in heaven is not willing that any of these little ones should be lost" (Mt. 18:14)

This story is used by Matthew to emphasise to his disciples the fact that God's love embraces even the juveniles in their midst. Children then had no rights, were defenceless and utterly helpless. They were unimportant and insignificant; excluded from the synagogues and were classed together with the weak of society. The parable teaches that the Good Shepherd is willing to search for even such as these.

THE LOST COIN

Jesus comes very near to upsetting the Pharisees' sensitivities yet again with this second story. He did not quite say "Which woman among you...?" but "A woman." It is enough, though, to raise the temperatures of these orthodox Jewish religious types simply by saying that a member of the fairer, but inferior, sex was the hero of his next story. Jesus again uses an outcast, in this case a "gender" outcast in his story. We have already seen the low view of women during the New Testament times in the parable of the Two Debtors. They were not taught the Law and could not participate in the synagogue services. They were classified together with children and were only expected to be active in domestic life.

Jesus changed that. He elevated womanhood and included them as citizens of the kingdom. Whilst women certainly had different roles to men, Jesus nevertheless gave them new opportunities they had never had before. For instance, women were the first witnesses of his resurrection, the most important event of history. The place of honour was given to a woman who alone anointed him before his death and burial. There were women who followed him and he seemed happy to allow Mary to sit at his feet to be taught.

The structure of this story is similar to that of the Good Shepherd. One coin is lost. She searches until she finds it. There is joy in the community over the restoration because she has found what was lost.

Scene 1: A woman has ten silver coins

These coins are drachmas, roughly equivalent to the price of a sheep. Money was a very rare commodity in those days, especially in a peasant environment largely making ends meet on subsistence farming and bartering. That meant the loss of one coin was very serious. If we had ten coins in our pockets and lost one we would not turn the house upside down looking for it. We would, however, if it was a valuable krugerand or gold coin.

Each coin was worth about a day's wage, so she was quite a poor woman. The coin would have been part of her jewellery or dowry. If she had been a Bedouin woman, she would have worn the coins on a chain around her veil, but a peasant woman like the one in this parable would have worn them on a necklace.

Scene 2: Seeking until she finds

Suddenly the necklace snaps. She manages to retrieve nine of the coins except one. She knows it is still in the house somewhere, but it is hard to see immediately where because the building has a low door and no windows. So she lights a lamp in the gloom and starts searching the rough floor. She uses a palm branch to gently sweep around, her ears straining for the sound of contact with the lost coin.

Because she has only ten coins, the loss of one represents a tenth. Jesus is seeking to intensify the value of the lost one here. Were it one in a hundred, she would not have felt so bad about it. Like the shepherd, the woman is determined to find what she has lost. And she does so.

Scene 3: Joy in the community

Having at last spotted the coin and grasped it gleefully, the woman calls her friends and neighbours to celebrate with her for finding what she had lost. It is personal joy shared with the community again, as with the shepherd and the lost sheep: "In the same way, I tell you, there is rejoicing in the presence of the angels of God over one sinner who repents" (vs. 10).

While the same themes are contained in all three parables in Luke chapter 15, each story differs in important details. Take the status of the seekers. In the Lost Sheep, he is a middle income man, while the seeker in the story of the lost coin is a poor woman. In the Lost Sons, the "seeker" is a rich man - the father. These different key people have the same determination to seek until the lost is found. In each story, Jesus wants his listeners to identify God as the seeker. Joy when the lost is found is another common thread. We will see in the next chapter the joy of the father when the Prodigal finally returns.

In the parable of the Lost Sheep, Jesus talks about one being lost out of a hundred, in the Lost Coin one out of ten and, in the Lost Sons, one out of two. With each parable, he is intensifying the value of what is lost. It is as if he is saying to the Pharisees: "You don't think one sheep out of a hundred is worth going after?

So what about one coin out of ten? What about one son out of two?" In each of these stories, there is a repentant sinner identified with what was lost.

THEMES OF THE PARABLE

In each story, God is pictured first as a shepherd, then as a woman and, finally, as the waiting father. There is an element of joy in all the stories - personal and communal. There is the attitude of the lost in this trio. The Jews knew that the lost sheep was a poor, helpless animal. The coin cannot help itself to return to the pile: it needs to be found. The Prodigal is "dead", eventually comes to his senses and finds his way back to his father. The lost are unable to help themselves. The seeker has to take the initiative. It is all of grace when the lost is found.

There is also the element of cost in the three parables: the cost to the shepherd as he goes out into the wilderness to find his sheep, carrying this burden on his shoulders; for the woman there is the cost involved in the long search, carefully and patiently carried out; and then there is the cost to the father as he waits day after day for his wayward son to return. In all these stories we see something of the Cross. If there is one statement that sums up these stories, it is this: "The Son of Man came to seek and to save what was lost" (Lk. 19:10).

6

THE LOST SONS
Luke 15:11-31

The father was aghast. He had never heard anything like it before. The temerity - and the devastating insult! His younger son had just marched boldly into his study and asked for his inheritance as soon as possible. He could not wait for his father to be on his deathbed for the share-out. He wanted his now. To add to the insult, he was going to sell off his share of the land so that he could go and have a good time on the Mediterranean Riviera. It would mean breaking up the estate the old man had carefully built up over the years into a really profitable business...

This really is the most beautifully crafted of all Jesus' stories. Traditionally it has been called the Prodigal Son, but as we shall see, we should look at it as the parable of the Lost Sons. There are two sons here and both were lost - one away from home, the other back on the family farm. Another perspective is that this is the story of the Waiting Father. Both of these titles would more accurately reflect the message of this parable. Jesus' stories are like diamonds - we can look at them from different angles and see something new and beautiful each time.

This parable can best be understood by dividing it into four scenes.

Scene 1: The broken relationship at home
The younger son's request for his share of the inheritance was unusual. It was also an unreasonable one and an extraordinary insult to his father. According to Old Testament customs, wills should only be made when a person is close to death, not when they are healthy. There is however a provision for an oral will to be made while they are still alive. Often that is done to protect property, so it can be reserved for whoever it is intended.

This oral will is made especially when a man plans to remarry and wants his children from his first marriage to have his inheritance. So to guard against his estate being seized by his second wife he is entitled by law to make a will. But the normal practice is for a man to make his will and divide his property only when he is near death. In 2 Kings 20:1, Isaiah tells the terminally ill King Hezekiah, "Put your house in order, for you are going to die." In other words, "Make a will." Look at this quote from a rabbi: "The day life draws to a close is the right time for giving one's property to son, wife, brother or friend, not during one's lifetime." This emphasises that inheritance is assigned at the point of death.

What is unusual about the Prodigal son's request is that he asked for his inheritance while his father was still fit and healthy. The request is rare even by Western standards. In Britain today, wills are commonly made while people are relatively young. But even here, we would only write the will, not actually give away the property at that stage.

Another factor to bear in mind is that, if the father did decide to divide his inheritance among members of his family, he retained the right to benefit from the estate while he was still alive. Even after handing over his possessions to his sons, he is entitled to live off the produce of the estate.

Understanding the Jewish laws on inheritance is important to make sense of the Prodigal's request. The Prodigal son's action is terribly insulting for three reasons. First, he requests the division of the inheritance. He does not just say, "Father, give me my share," but demands that the estate be carved up. Second, he also requests the full rights to dispose of his inheritance. It is not enough for this young man to receive the title deeds of the estate - he wants the right to sell the estate and use the profits to go far away and spend it on himself. That is most unusual. As long as the father is still alive, the Mishna (Jewish law) gives him the right to continue to benefit from his inheritance even after he had given it away to his sons. If this young man was now to take the title deeds of the estate, sell the land and take the money with him, how was the father going to live? These two requests, unheard of in the culture of the day, was the son's way of saying: "Father, I wish you were dead." That is the ultimate insult to a Middle Eastern father.

Third, in making these unusual requests, the Prodigal was also relinquishing his responsibilities as a son. All Middle Eastern sons were expected to grow up in the family home and join the father's business. Eventually they would run it. So this young man's desire to sell the land and clear off made the insult even more outrageous.

Jesus' listeners must have wondered what sort of story he was crafting because this scenario is most unusual, particularly in a Middle Eastern context. No son could make this sort of request and expect it to be received sympathetically. But amazingly the father agrees to it! David Pawson has called this parable the Prodigal Father, because he should not have given in to his son's absurd request! In Middle Eastern culture the son's totally insulting audacity was expected to be answered by the father picking him up, slapping him on his cheeks, calling him an idle, good-for-nothing son and throwing him out of the house. That was what the listeners of the parables expected Jesus to say, but to their horror our Lord said that the son was to be given what he wanted.

It was a unique act of love by the father. It is a picture of the divine action of God, because no human father would have done this. There is no more dramatic illustration of a love which grants freedom to a person, even though he has rejected and insulted the Giver, the creator Father God.

It grips the attention of the listeners. They must have wondered how the story was going to work out. The shepherd searching for his sheep and the woman looking for her coin were actions to be expected, but the action of the father was unprecedented. It is a picture of the love of God himself for mankind.

What is so easily missed in reading such a familiar parable is the silence of the eldest son. In Eastern cultures, the eldest son has an important role to play in the family. He is expected to protest about the father's action and refuse his share of the inheritance. It is not just the younger son who gets his share of the inheritance at this point. The eldest son receives his double portion, equivalent to two thirds of the property at the same time. He gains a lot from the share-out. Instead of doing the expected and honourable thing by refusing his inheritance at this time, he says nothing and receives it.

The eldest son is also expected to be a conciliator in family conflicts and crises. He is expected to take his brother out of the house, grab him by the lapels, slap his face, rough him up a bit and tell him not to be so stupid and go and apologise to his father for insulting and upsetting him! The fact that the eldest son was silent suggests that his relationships with his father as well as with his brother were already broken. With a minimum of words, Jesus paints a picture of a home with broken relationships.

I remember on one occasion when my youngest brother innocently asked one of our uncles how much our father was worth in monetary terms. When word about this reached my father, he was furious. To make matters worse, my brother then proceeded to purchase a large life insurance policy for which he had no means of paying. Unwittingly, he had insulted my father in the same way as the prodigal. My role as the eldest son was to pacify my father and speak strongly to my brother. This parable has a very familiar feel indeed!

There is an important Middle Eastern custom in connection with this parable called the *kezazah*, which literally means "*cutting off.*" The Jews are very particular about two things which, if violated, could result in the perpetrator being cut off from the people. In such cases the *kezazah* ceremony would be performed on the offender. One such offence is marrying a Gentile. The second, equally serious, is if you lose your land, property or your inheritance to Gentiles. The *kezazah* ceremony involved smashing an earthenware jar full of parched corn and nuts in front of the offender and proclaiming, "So and so is cut off from his people!" When the ceremony was over, that person became an outcast. Even if he was destitute and starving, no one from the village would help him. *Kezazah* reflects the great Jewish sense of solidarity of the extended family and community, in contrast to the individualism of the West. An insult to one member of the family was an insult to the whole community.

This "cutting off" is similar to modern situations where someone is treated as dead if he denies his original faith and converts to another religion. In Jewish and Muslim circles, a mock funeral may be conducted by parents for children who have converted to another faith to signify that they are "dead" and are "cut off" from them. This reflects the strong sense of solidarity to one's community and faith. The Prodigal has not done anything yet to warrant the *kezazah* ceremony. But when he returns in rags and empty-handed, they would all know that he has lost everything to Gentiles and they would have to decide whether to carry out the *kezazah* ceremony on him.

Meanwhile the community would have been angered by the Prodigal as he went around the village trying to sell his land. In the Middle East, selling land is a long and protracted business. Land is far more important there than in the West, where we treat it as an impersonal asset. Land in the East is part of the owner's identity because it has been handed down from generation to generation. The whole Middle East conflict is over the issue of land.

To sell land that had been passed down and inherited was an extremely contentious issue. So the Prodigal would have encountered fierce opposition when knocking on doors and asking people if they were interested in buying his property. His action would reveal that he had insulted his father and the whole village would close ranks against him.

In this first scene then, Jesus describes a family crisis where relationships had broken down. This scene is full of tension and drama. There is the prodigal's unreasonable request, the father's unusual consent and the eldest son's unexpected silence. The scene is set. The audience want to hear more.

Scene 2: Leaving home

Jesus tells the story so that the younger son finally manages to sell the land he has inherited and then disappears over the horizon - to an unexpected tragedy. The "distant country" the lad went to was

85

probably Antioch, the Paris of the East during the time of Jesus. He wanted fun and excitement, so that was the obvious place to go. Significantly, the first Gentile Church was started in Antioch. The Good News is really for sinners!

In Antioch the younger son blows his money through "wild living" according to the story. There is no mention of prostitutes; it is the eldest son who mentions them. His money disappears just as a severe famine struck the land - a frequent enough disaster in those days. He becomes utterly destitute. So he does what is common in such circumstances: he finds a wealthy man to attach himself to.

"Attach" is a lovely word here. It means to "glue" oneself to the rich man. The latter must have felt he was being sucked by a leech, so desperate was the need of the son who had thrown everything away in his short time of pleasure. In the East it is impolite to say "No" to such requests, as we have seen in the parable of the Banquet. Undesirables are got rid of by offering them the most unpleasant jobs in the hope that they would refuse the offer and go away. This young man is asked to feed the pigs on the estate. For a Jewish boy you cannot have a worse job than that! However, his desperation is such that he takes the job, despite it being against his religion, dignity and everything else.

What is a nice Jewish boy doing, feeding pigs? Well, he is not so nice any more. This really would have outraged and revolted Jesus' listeners. A Jewish boy from a wealthy family has sunk so low that he is feeding pigs for a Gentile pig farmer! He cannot sink any lower. His contact with unclean animals could mean the loss of his Jewishness. What does this mean? The word "Jew" is the English transliteration of Hebrew *Y'hudi* which means "to give thanks, to praise and to confess openly." To be a true Jew is to be someone who gives thanks and praise to God and has a close relationship with God. (How appropriate then, that one of the greatest British musicians is Sir Yehudi Menuhin) Contact with pigs would mean that the prodigal would lose his closeness with God. By this act, he has brought further shame to his father and his community.

It is one of the many twists in this story which would have left his listeners agog, dying to know how it would end. Not content with telling them that this Jewish boy stooped so low that he began looking after pigs, Jesus rubs it in by saying he was so hungry that he would have eaten the same pods he was giving the pigs! There is humour here even in this most outrageous part of the story.

There are two types of carob pods in the Middle East - the wild and the Syrian varieties. The latter is sweet and is nutritious, but the wild type grows on a thorny bush and has no nutritious value whatsoever. Its fruits are black and taste awful. Even if you were hungry, eating this wild carob pod would do the stomach no good. They are only worth feeding the pigs with. The problem was that it was the pods or hardly anything else, for Jesus said "no one gave him anything" to eat. In other words, no one was feeding the young man regularly. Famine was in the land and there were lots of cheap labourers around. The well-off had no obligation to feed them as well as their own families. Occasionally the boss would throw some scraps of food to his workers. The pig-owner would have occasionally slaughtered one of the herd and given the less desirable parts of the animal to his servants. But would a well brought up Jewish young man eat pork even if he was starving? Jesus leaves this to the imagination of his listeners but invites them to identify with the prodigal. That is how God sees us.

In such dire straits, facing death from hunger, the son makes an unexpected "repentance." It is not a true repentance, as we will see when we understand his well thought-out speech to his father. He intends to say: "Father, I have sinned against heaven and in your sight I am no longer worthy to be called your son; make me like one of your hired servants."

There are three types of servant in the Middle East. There is the *doulos*, literally a slave. He has been bought and bonded, but he is also part of the estate and almost part of the family. Another category is the *paides*, slaves of an even lower class who perform the menial work. A third type is the *misthioi* or hired servants. They live outside the family in the village and are employed on contract. A hired servant has no personal interest in the running of the estate or his temporary master. His position is precarious. Being self-employed, he depended on work being available. If there was none, he was in trouble. But a hired servant has the advantage of being free and independent. In his prepared speech, the younger son was going to ask his father to make him a hired servant. Being a hired servant rather than a slave would have meant he could live in the village instead of with his father and brother. He could earn his way and possibly repay the money he had lost. In other words he wants no grace and no favours from anyone. He wants to pay his way independently and will not ask for charity.

In this scene then, we have the prodigal's unexpected tragedy and his unexpected repentance described. This is turning out to be some story.

Scene 3: The homecoming

The younger son is seeking to return home with some dignity intact. But he has three big problems. The first is that he had grossly insulted his father by asking for his inheritance, in effect telling him that he wished he was dead. He has sold the property and squandered all the proceeds on pleasure far away from home. Now he is forced to go back and face the consequences. He decides to acknowledge that he has sinned. That will be expected of him and he hopes it will pacify his father. His confession is probably not true repentance yet - just a way of getting out of the mess he is in.

The second problem is his brother. The eldest son has received two-thirds of his father's inheritance in accordance with Jewish law. Big brother now legally owns everything, so if the younger son goes back home he would be there courtesy of his brother's hospitality. He will have to eat his brother's food. That will be extremely hard because of their broken relationship. The Prodigal will have to eat humble pie and live off his brother's share of the estate. Being a hired servant will get round that particular problem.

The third problem is the village. His return there will be humiliating. He can expect a hostile reception. He will have to face the threat of the *kezazah*. The mob will be after his blood once the returning traveller has been spotted by the "bush telegraph" of the day - little boys loitering around the village who ran around and told everybody who they had seen coming down the road. Not only will he face verbal and physical abuse and the threat of the *kezazah*, the villagers might even try to prevent him going home so that he would not embarrass and hurt his father a second time.

But the news has reached the father as well as the villagers. Jesus tells us that "while he was still a long way off, his father saw him." What is the father expected to do now? He can see the boy is dishevelled and in rags. He knows his son has lost everything as he had said he would. An Oriental father is now expected to explode with anger and deal severely with his son who has so insulted and humiliated him by his actions. This is what the listeners would expect to happen next.

Incredibly, Jesus says that instead of being filled with anger the father is "filled with compassion for him!" We have already encountered this word "compassion" in the parable of the Good Samaritan. There, as here, we are to hear echoes of God's strong feelings for his people through the story.

The father has to act fast because he is fully aware of how his son will be treated. The phrase "while he was still a long way off, his father saw him" is intended to show that this father was broken-hearted over his son and looked out for his return every day. He is the Waiting Father. He runs to the edge of the village to meet the hungry, filthy young man in tattered clothes for a highly public reconciliation. His race to get there is most unusual in itself and humiliating. Old Middle Eastern noblemen do not run in public. It was not easy to do so in the long, flowing robes which they wore. It meant lifting the hems to the middle of the thighs and revealing their underwear in the process. Everyone who saw the old man doing this would have sniggered. This is most unusual and everyone is shocked by the father's humiliating action. But the father has to do it to enable his son to enter the village under his protection from a hostile crowd. So violence against the Prodigal was prevented and the possibility of the dreaded *kezazah* avoided.

It is vital to see that it is the father who takes the initiative. In this we see the action of God himself. The son had been prepared to run the gauntlet. But to his utter amazement and disbelief he sees his father running towards him. Instead of the anticipated ruthless hostility which he thoroughly deserved and expected, he is overwhelmed by love. The father has run the gauntlet and publicly humiliated himself to meet his son before he was harmed by the angry villagers. The prodigal experiences an unexpected demonstration of love and forgiveness.

As his father reaches him with his arms outstretched in joyous greeting, the son launches into his carefully prepared speech: "Father, I have sinned against heaven and against you. I am no longer worthy to be called your son" and that is as far as he gets. The father interrupts him and says, "Be quiet! That's enough. There's no need to say any more." The prodigal never got as far as asking to be employed as a hired servant. After what he has just witnessed he could not complete his prepared speech. To do so would have been seen as spurning his father's generous action. It is only really at this point that Jesus wants us to see the Prodigal's true repentance. He understands now the deep, deep love the father has for him. He realises that he cannot do anything about his own restoration. It is all down to grace.

The father now does a number of unexpected and beautiful things. First, he embraces his wayward son and kisses him - again and again. Contrary to what some commentators believe, this is not the sign of equality, but of reconciliation and forgiveness. After a serious quarrel, part of the act of reconciliation is a public kiss by the people involved in the dispute. No matter how old the son is in Middle Eastern culture, the son is never his father's equal. He is always a son. Notice also the father does not complain about the awful smell of pigs emanating from the prodigal! He is not told to go and clean up before the father would kiss him.

This is an unusual demonstration of love. The reaction of Jesus' listeners to the parable would be: "Wow! Where do you find a father like that?" There is no earthly father like that. But this is what the Heavenly Father is like. This extravagant love is extraordinary and unheard-of in an Oriental culture.

The father calls for the best robe to be brought out for his son. This was the father's best robe which he wore at big parties. When the guests arrive at the party to congratulate the father, they will see the son in his father's robe and know that he has been restored to his family.

A signet ring is also given to the Prodigal. It was a seal of authority in the house, signifying that the son is to be trusted in a remarkable way. The servants were then told to put shoes on the son. Slaves did not wear shoes - only free men and women did. Those shoes were a sign that the servants were now to accept the son as their master. When guests arrived at a house like this they were expected to take their shoes off. But the master walks into the house with his shoes on. Expecting to return as a servant, the prodigal finds himself accepted as a son.

The father shows further extraordinary generosity and joy by having a fatted calf killed and cooked for a celebration feast. "For this son of mine was dead and is alive again; he was lost and is found" (Lk. 15:23-24). Only a fatted calf would do for this occasion because it was big enough to feed over a hundred people and Jesus wants us to understand that the father wanted to share his joy with the whole community. He invites everyone along to his party. He wants his boy restored to the community. It was a great honour for the Prodigal. Cows were not normally killed for feasting because they were useful for milk. This shows the joy and generosity of the father and Jesus intends us to see in this the love of the Heavenly Father. So then the prodigal experiences an extraordinary and an extravagant welcome by the father. No recriminations or condemnation. Only reconciliation and restoration to the family and the community.

The story could have ended with the prodigal son being greeted by his father and welcomed home. The listeners would have been satisfied. There was certainly sufficient drama up to that point to make a good story. Jesus, however, chooses to embellish it to demonstrate the extraordinary way in which the boy was being publicly restored as a son, not as a servant. And in this he wants his listeners to know that that is the kind of welcome they can expect from God if they return to him. He wants to receive us back as sons, not servants. The story could have ended here with the big party, with music, dancing and feasting. After all, everyone likes a happy ending to their stories. But Jesus uses his stories not for sentimental reasons but for the purpose of teaching truths and challenging his listeners to faith. Having invited his listeners to identify themselves so far with the prodigal son, he now directs the second part of the story to the Pharisees and the teachers of the Law.

Scene 4: The eldest son's rejection

The eldest son's role in this story is often overlooked and is usually untold. Jesus now brings him into the story and he wants his listeners to contrast the two sons. The younger son had insulted his father. Now the eldest son insults him in an equally extraordinary way. This son had been working away on the farm and was on his way home when he heard music and dancing. It signalled the start of a celebration, for in the Middle East music preceded the meal, not the other way round. The start of the music was the call to the feast. People came in, started dancing and then sat down to eat.

When the eldest son heard the music he asked someone what was going on. No doubt he could smell the meat being cooked and is suspicious. If he had a good relationship with his father he would have gone straight into the house and asked what the celebration was about. The father would have said, "Your brother has come back," to which would have come an enthusiastic response like, "Oh! Isn't that wonderful!" He would have embraced his brother and got into the swing of the party. But this does not happen here.

Eastern custom required the presence of the eldest son at a banquet. He was to play host at any party given by his father. He was expected to stand barefoot at the door and welcome the guests. It was the father's way of saying, "My older son is your servant." Instead the eldest son refuses to enter. This is just as insulting to his father as his younger brother's request for his share of the inheritance. The father has therefore been insulted by both sons.

An Oriental father is now expected to be angry at this insulting behaviour. Instead this father responds by going out of the house for the second time that day, this time to plead with his eldest son to come to the feast. Again the father takes the initiative. It is extremely unusual for a Middle Eastern father to do that. He was prepared to humble and humiliate himself for a second time in one day. Jesus' listeners would have exclaimed: "We've never heard of a father who has done that before!" In this we are to see a picture of the heavenly Father. No earthly father can love in this way.

What is expected of the eldest son now? Even if he wants to quarrel with his father, he is still expected to enter the house and fulfil his role as a host first. This would include publicly embracing and welcoming his brother, receiving the congratulations offered to him and his father for the Prodigal's safe return and honouring his brother as the party's principal guest. He would be expected to do all this even if he has to grit his teeth. Only when the party is over and all the guests have gone home may he complain about the way his brother has been welcomed. This is the way of Oriental face-saving.

But the eldest son chooses to publicly humiliate his father by quarrelling as the guests are arriving. Middle East customs demand that the authority of the father (and mother, too) be held in high esteem, which makes the eldest son's actions such a terrible insult. The insults of both sons make the father's welcome even more remarkable. The father was expected to deal with the elder son's behaviour by ignoring him and proceeding with the banquet without him - outwardly smiling, being the perfect host but seething with anger inside. Afterwards he was expected to mete out punishment for this son's public insolence. But instead of rebuking, he pleads in yet another remarkable demonstration of love. In all the Middle Eastern literature ever written, it would be hard to find a story of a father who loved in this way. This is a picture of divine love.

In the face of such unexpected love and humility, the eldest son is now expected to apologise to the father and follow him into the house and join in the party. But despite knowing that it is unusually remarkable for a Middle Eastern nobleman to leave a banquet and plead for his oldest son to come in, he remains stubbornly unmoved. And he lets fly a barrage of criticism.

He does not even address his father. Whenever somebody is addressed throughout this parable, there is a title - except in this instance. There is no "Father..." This is regarded as extreme rudeness in Oriental societies. He moans: "I've been slaving for you ..." showing the state of his relationship with his father. His attitude is more of a slave than a son. He adds that he has never disobeyed his father's orders. Jesus throws that in for the Pharisees who claim they have obeyed all the laws, not like the sinners and tax collectors. But the son is being disobedient to his father by refusing to go into the house to play his traditional role as a host. He has insulted his father and broken the commandment that he should honour his father. He has broken the commandment of love - and Jesus intended the Pharisees to hear that. They claimed not to have broken any commandments but Jesus told them that they had broken the supreme commandment - to love your God with all your heart and all your mind and to love your neighbour as yourself.

The father is further accused of favouritism. He has never even given a young goat to the eldest son to have a party with his friends, yet the youngest son who has lost his share of the inheritance comes home to a feast with a fatted calf. "It's not fair!" is a frequent cry among children in the family - and one which is hard to deal with. This parable, however, shows that the father is fair. He goes out to forgive the youngest son and then a second time to win the eldest son.

By his action, the eldest son effectively cuts himself off from his family. Sa'id, a Middle Eastern theologian, in his commentary on Luke, says this brilliantly: "The older son shows disgust with his father's house. In saying that he would have liked to 'make merry with my friends'... he is no better than the Prodigal son who took his portion and travelled to a far country. The difference between them is that the Prodigal son is an honourable sinner in that he was perfectly open to his father. He told his father all that was in his heart. But the older brother was a hypocritical saint because he hid his feelings in his heart. He remained in the house all the while hating his father. He denies any relationship to his brother and thereby denies any relationship to his father. He says 'This is your son' rather than 'This is my brother.' With this statement the older son removed himself from the family and passed judgement of "outcast" upon himself." Having a Middle Eastern concept and understanding of the family, Sa'id comments that in those words the elder son effectively said, "I don't belong to this family." That is how serious some of these statements are understood in a Middle Eastern context.

The eldest son reveals his own concept of joy - having a barbecue with his friends, but not rejoicing at the return of his brother "from the dead." He attacks his younger brother by accusing him of spending his inheritance on prostitutes, which was never mentioned in the first part of the story. The eldest son also uses the phrase "your" wealth rather than "his" money. He is trying to drive a wedge between his father and his younger brother. In effect the elder brother is saying, "Don't you realise what he's done, Father? He has lost your wealth. You can't trust him with anything any more!"

The father is expected to be furious at this unjustified criticism. A son just does not speak to a Middle Eastern father like that! The father, however, does not react with anger, but addresses this son with a title, "My child ..." The Greek word is *teknon*, a term of endearment, a conciliatory word. It is a remarkable word to use after all the verbal abuse the father has endured. "These words really come out of a wounded, suffering heart, because the father longed to have his joy complete in that he would be greatly pleased to see his two sons together in his house. The love that knows no weariness makes such a gracious announcement" (Sa'id).

The father pleads with his son to join in the rejoicing. There is a contrast here. The father ran out with joy in his heart to greet his returning younger son. But when he went out to the eldest son it with a heaviness of heart. It seemed that he knew this son's true character. It is another snipe at the hardened, hypocritical Pharisees. God is reaching out to these self-righteous, legalistic types, too.

The father assures the eldest son that his rights are fully protected: "Everything I have is yours." The Prodigal received and squandered a third of the inheritance, but the rest is owned by the elder brother. He is the master, the heir.

Kenneth Bailey constructs the conversation between father and son in this way:

Older son: You never gave me a kid, father.

Father: All that I have is yours.

Older son: Yes, but I don't have the right of disposition. I own everything but I still can't slaughter a goat and have a feast with my friends.

Father: Oh, I see. You also want me dead!

The conversation does not get that far, but it was heading in that direction. The prodigal brother was granted the right to sell off his share of the property and spend the money on living it up. The elder brother was saying in a less transparent way, that he wanted the same thing. We need to see that both sons were saying, in effect: "Father, we wish you would drop dead!"

The father says: "He is your brother..." The father does not apologise for the banquet nor rebuke his older son, but cries from his heart for understanding. He wants him to understand that despite the Prodigal squandering all that wealth he is still his brother and he has a right to be restored to the family.

The parable has no ending. The eldest son is still outside the house. Jesus has left it to the listeners' imagination to make their own conclusions. And he leaves it to the Pharisees to decide whether they will come in and join the banquet with the other sinners or stay outside. He leaves them with a challenge. We, too, have to decide whether to come in and accept this extraordinary welcome from the Father or stand outside and sulk.

What a remarkable story this is! Having said that the story could have ended earlier with the prodigal's acceptance, this is certainly the "wrong" place to end it now. Jesus leaves the story dangling in suspense. His listeners would have gone away discussing the part of the eldest son more than that of the prodigal. But this is good story-telling and suits the purposes that Jesus intended.

THEMES OF THE PARABLE

How does one summarise such an incredible story?

First, Jesus tells us what it means to be lost. The traditional view of this parable is that the Prodigal son is lost. But as we have seen, there were two sons and both were lost. One is lost away from home (like the Lost Sheep), the other at home (like the Lost Coin). Jesus is saying to the Pharisees that they can be lost as a sinner away from God or as a sinner right inside God's house. We can be in church and be religious but still be lost. What God is really interested in is a relationship with us as sons. Even if we are religious, our relationship can be that of a slave rather than as a son. The Pharisees in their slavish observance of the Law and their good works related to God as slaves. Jesus appeals to them to come as sons.

Second, this story teaches us about repentance. It is defined in the parable as coming to one's senses, seeing our unworthiness and turning to the Father. There is the lovely picture of the son saying, "I know I stink, that I have shamed my family and my village, but I will return to my father and say that I have sinned." God accepts us as we are - warts and all. The younger son repents - the older son does not.

When we repent, who actually does the repenting? Is it God who draws us or is it man who comes to his senses and makes that first move? The Bible says it is both. We have to turn and then God will turn to us. The rabbis taught that as we turn, God turns with us. And that is what we see in the picture of the father running out to the Prodigal. He sees him coming to the village and runs out to meet him halfway. Man turns and as he does so, he discovers that God turns and runs out to greet him.

Third, this is an amazing portrayal of grace. We see the patient waiting and longing of the father. Grace is costly - he runs out of his house to greet the Prodigal and leaves the banquet to plead with the eldest son. The father humbles and humiliates himself twice to welcome both sons. This parable is, therefore, rightly called The Waiting Father, because he waits and waits for his sons to return. It is the father who takes the initiative, and Jesus wants us to see that we cannot save ourselves. It is all of grace.

Fourth, like the Lost Sheep and Lost Coin, there is a strong note of joy in this story. Personal and communal joy. The joy of the father is to be shared. When we return to God our Father, not only is there personal joy in the heart of God, we are told the angels will join in with the celebrations.

Fifth, this parable also speaks to us about sonship. One son is lost and welcomed back as a son. The other son stays a servant. That reflects their attitudes to the father. Do we relate to God as Father or as a tyrant? The Prodigal's attitude to his father is as a father, but the older son's attitude is that the father is more of a bad master.

SUMMARY

This is a powerful story of a father and two sons. Both grossly insulted the father and wanted him dead. Both broke the father's heart. In both cases the father came out to meet them in unique expressions of generous love. The Prodigal son responds, repents and is restored to sonship. The eldest son refuses to repent despite the father's pleading. He insults his father publicly, showing that he was as lost as his brother was when he left home for a distant country.

The Pharisees are challenged to see themselves as the eldest son. Jesus pleads with them through this story not to stand outside and sulk, but to soften their hearts and come to the banquet. Just as they have a right to be there as the "eldest son", sinners, too, have the right to be there as the "prodigal son." The parable paints a priceless picture of God as the waiting Father, patient, forgiving, understanding, gentle, broken-hearted, humble and humiliated. It is a picture of Jesus himself and his sacrifice on the Cross for us. The father leaves the house and humiliates himself in a public demonstration of unexpected and undeserved love.

Jesus says we are one of the two lost sons. Which one are you?

7

THE PRUDENT STEWARD
Luke 16:1-15

He was in a tight corner. He had been told to clear his desk. No job and the unlikelihood of getting anything suitable in the future either. Unless he could come up with something brilliant. As he sat there, cogitating in the candlelight, it suddenly hit him: huge discounts for the tenant farmers! First thing next morning he called these men in. Flabbergasted, they accepted and paid up on the spot. When the master heard about it, a broad smile crossed his face and he could be heard chuckling about the cheek of his ex-estate manager.

Flutter the leaves of the calendar and the scene switches from the Israel of Jesus' day to Britain in the late twentieth century. A bank executive responsible for a number of business accounts is called into his boss's office and dismissed for negligence. He goes to his computer, picks out an account and phones the person. "Your overdraft is £500,000, but I'm reducing it to £300,000. He rings another one: "Your overdraft is £100,000. We'll bring it down to £50,000." Then he clears his desk and leaves ...

There are two parables about money in Luke chapter 16. The first is the Prudent Steward and the second is the Rich Man and Lazarus. Sandwiched between these two parables are some teachings about money. Both stories begin with "There was a rich man ..." In both stories the present is contrasted with the future. *How* one lives now will affect *where* one lives in the future. The Prudent Steward is about a "good" bad man whereas the Rich Man and Lazarus is about a "bad" rich man.

Let us look now at the first of these "money parables." I first thought this story should be called The Unrighteous Steward. That, in fact, is what it is called in some Bibles. This is probably one of the most difficult parables in the gospels. Its contents have been argued over as long as Bible commentators have been around!

The traditional interpretation is that the steward acted corruptly throughout - falsification of accounts, cheating his master and lying to the tenants. All the corrupt business practices are here. Even such a highly respected commentator as C.C. Torrey takes this view: "This passage brings before us a new Jesus, one who is inclined to compromise with evil. He approves a program of canny self-interest ... He bases the teaching on the story of a shrewd scoundrel who feathered his own nest at the expense of the man who trusted him and then appears to say to his disciples, "Let this be your model!"

Is this the way we should view the story or is there another way of doing so? The difficulties of the parables are twofold. First, Jesus holds up this man as a model for us, for he says at the end of the story: "Look at what this man has done with unrighteous money. You should do the same." But to suggest that we go out and act corruptly does not ring true of the person of Jesus. The second problem is the advice in verse 9: "... use worldly wealth to gain friends for yourselves ..." It is jarring verses like these that have caused me to avoid this parable for a long time. The key question to understanding this parable is: Was the steward committing a fraud by his action? If so then the tenants were accomplices to the crime and Jesus had used the criminal actions of the steward as an example. Alternatively, if the steward's action was not criminal, then Jesus is commending his prudence as an example for his disciples to whom the parable is addressed. Although the Pharisees are likely to have been within earshot because comments towards the end are addressed to them, this parable is primarily intended for his own disciples.

The only way we can understand this parable is again through looking at the Oriental background. An important part of this background to the parable is the absentee landlord. Such men were common enough - they owned land but lived elsewhere. The landlord in this parable pays the site a visit and calls the steward to a meeting to enquire what was going on, especially why this employee was squandering his possessions.

The steward is a legal agent. The Greek word for "steward"

could mean "head servant" - responsible for the welfare and discipline of the household staff (Luke 12:42). The man could be a city treasurer (Rm. 16:23) or an estate manager, as he is in this story. He is a legally appointed man instructed by his absent master to look after his land and tenants, to collect the rent and make sure the business is run properly. He is the master's representative.

In the Middle Eastern way of doing things, the estate manager is expected to receive a "kick back" when he carried out a transaction - something "under the table". This greasing of the palm was a customary way of doing business in that part of the world, an accepted way of life. It still is! The Chinese call it *ang pow* (red packet) or "tea money". At every Chinese New Year, law enforcement officers go round the businesses with New Year greetings and before leaving receive *ang pow* packets stuffed with money. In Malaysia it is called "*kopi* money" - meaning money for buying coffee.

The steward received this kind of money and other perks. At festival times he would receive gratuities. All these are off-the-record payments, so they would not appear on the bills. The bills would only list the exact amounts owed to the master on them.

Scene 1: The steward's unexpected dismissal

The master's reputation has been damaged. He is assumed to be an upright man. This is consistent with the contrast between good and bad in the stories of the Lost Sons and the Rich Man and Lazarus. Jesus has a habit of using a righteous man and a rogue in his stories. If the master was not a man of integrity, but was cruel and wicked, he would not have merely fired the steward. He would have punished him physically as well.

Presumably news of the steward's mishandling of his affairs reaches the master when he comes home from a journey. Although the report is primarily about the steward, by implication it casts a shadow on the master's own reputation. The parable portrays a master who is not around much, leaving his business affairs to be managed by employees. He appears to be too trusting, as evidenced by the steward's actions.

The steward has neglected his duty. It is not fraud, because he has not run off with any money. If it were misappropriation of funds, he would have been thrown into jail and asked to repay the money. Instead it is waste resulting from his over consumption. It is negligence because of his laziness. The phrase "wasting his possessions" is the same as that which was used in the parable of the Lost Sons. The steward has squandered his master's possessions in a similar way the Prodigal son did with his share of his father's inheritance. After all, the master is not around to check on his high-flying life-style.

The steward's activities reflect badly on the master. That is the way it is regarded in the East and to a certain extent in the West. Honour is of paramount importance in the Middle East. Lose that honour and you have lost everything. It is what the Chinese call "face"- a matter of honour. The master has lost "face" through the steward's activities. He is a laughing stock in the community because of what the steward has done in his absence. Everyone knows about the steward's activities except the master.

The steward is called into the master's office and given the sack. Again we have to understand that Oriental masters have enormous power. The steward is told to put the accounts in order and surrender the books. This was an unexpected predicament. What is the steward expected to do now? Jesus' listeners would have expected the steward to loudly protest his innocence and then, if that failed to move the master, he would plead for mercy: "Please, please, I've got a wife and children to support ..." Amazingly, the steward stays silent.

This says, firstly, that he is guilty. He also knows his master has found out the truth and that excuses will not get him his job back. In a strange sort of way, his silence implies that there is a degree of nobleness in him. It is sickening to hear people caught red-handed for some crime or misdemeanour like theft, fraud, wastefulness or negligence protesting their innocence. The steward knows that his dismissal was just and that his master was fair in his judgement.

The master could have had the steward beaten and thrown out. At the very least he should, by right, have given his wayward employee a severe dressing down. All this was the normal Oriental way of justice for such a crime in Jesus' day. His master, however, waives his right to inflict any punishment on his errant employee. So while the steward experiences the master's judgement, he also, amazingly, experiences his boss's mercy. He gets off very lightly.

This shows us something of the master's character. He is very demanding but he is also merciful, even to a wasteful, lazy, negligent steward. We in the West tend to overlook this mercy of the master when reading this story, but it is vital that we understand it.

Scene 2: The steward's unusual plan

The steward has a big problem. He has just been sacked from a lucrative, comfortable job and was highly unlikely to get a similar one. He thinks about manual labour but decides he is not strong enough to dig and he is too ashamed to beg. The idea of becoming a labourer is degrading to an educated man in his position. "What! Sweating away in all that muck!" In any case, manual labour was considered menial and looked down upon in the East. It would be too demeaning for this fired estate manager.

He now has a damaged reputation and in desperation, he hits on a daring plan to repair it. It is a gamble in which he risks everything on the master's mercy. It will mean jail if he fails; if he succeeds, he will be the hero of the community and, most important, he will be able to land himself another job. He realises that the way to restore his reputation and honour is to restore his master's reputation and honour. Success of his plan would mean that he would be hailed as a shrewd man and he could hold his head high again and, most important, get the kind of job in keeping with his restored reputation. That is why he thinks: "I know what I'll do so that, when I lose my job here, people will welcome me into their houses" (vs. 4). Drastic action has to be taken now to secure his future. Otherwise it will be too late.

His plan was to reduce the tenants' debts. The key to this is that no one knows he has been fired yet. So he must act quickly. He has the debtors summoned - men who are relatively rich and important, judging by the amounts they owe his master. Harvest time, when the debts are normally due to be settled, has not arrived yet, so the summonses must mean something important needs to be discussed. And the steward sees these men individually.

The fact that the tenants responded to the summonses showed that they believed the steward was still acting on his master's authority. There is no indication that they knew what was going on or that they were colluding with the steward. The consequences would have been very severe if they were found to be dealing with him knowing that he had been dismissed. The relationship between landlord and tenant in the Middle East is an extremely important one based on trust.

In Jesus' time, there were three types of tenants: those who paid a percentage of their crop to the landlord; those who paid rent in cash; and those who paid an agreed portion of the crop. The latter fits the story best. The debts are declared as oil and wheat. One tenant was given a fifty per cent oil reduction and the other a twenty per cent wheat reduction - significant discounts! Both reductions were roughly equivalent to fifty denarii. One denarii was quite a large amount of money. Between a hundred and three hundred denarii amounted to a year's salary, so the rents in this story were high.

Having been asked how much they owed and then given these reductions, each of these tenants was handed their bill and told: "OK, now sit down and quickly change it to the new amount in your own writing." This is very important, for Jewish law stipulates that a legal document is only valid when written in a person's own handwriting. If the steward had altered the bill himself, it would have been fraud.

The tenants were not suspicious about these generous reductions because negotiations about rental based on crops is an ongoing affair in the Middle East. Haggling over the price is a way of life - no one pays the agreed amount. With rent it is exactly the same. There is always a reason or excuse why, when payment is due to the landlord, that the tenant should pay less. "What about the tree that was blown down during that big storm? The harvest is poor this year because of too much rain ... drought ... pests ... a bad lot of fertiliser ... too many weeds ..." Bargaining was and is a way of life in the East.

Part of the steward's responsibility was to regularly go out into the fields to find out what was going on, so that when the tenants came up with their excuses at the end of harvest, the master could check with the steward to see if they were real reasons for reductions. The steward needed to walk a tightrope all the time. On one hand he was in his master's pay, but on the other hand the tenants regularly greased his palm. He had to keep both sides happy all the time.

Instead of waiting until harvest time to have long haggling sessions with the master, suddenly these tenants are called to the steward and informed of big reductions in the year's rental. They are impressed and delighted: "What a good man you are, steward! And what a generous master you have! You've done a good job steward - you've represented us well to the master and he's heard your plea ..." Suspicion does not cross their minds because this kind of haggling was common practice in the Middle East.

The plan succeeds. The steward gets the credit for arranging the reductions, the master's honour is restored and the steward's reputation rockets, at least with these tenants. The steward has not done anything illegal and the tenants are not involved in a conspiracy to defraud the master. There is no hint either that the steward pocketed the difference.

Some scholars believe there is an indication here that the original accounts included the interest due on the deferred payment. Worked out on an annual basis, rent is payable at the end of the year (end of harvest) and the master could rightly charge interest for that 12-month period which could be included in the account. But Old Testament scriptures show that God forbids the charging of interest. This, however, did not stop the Jews who devised ingenious ways of getting round the Law. It has been suggested that this steward took off the interest element. This is possible but I believe unlikely, given the large discounts involved. Other scholars believe this interest was the steward's commission.

He decided to forego his own profit so that the master would not lose anything. This paying out of his own pocket, in effect, would restore both men's reputations and the steward could get another job. Again this is unlikely in view of the sums involved. No steward receives a fifty or twenty per cent commission for managing his master's estate. What is more likely is that the master and the steward would have already agreed the minimum rental for each of his tenants. A "base line" would have been established beforehand in advance of final negotiations with the tenants. The steward knows what the master is prepared to accept. This would have been the common practice. The discounts offered by the steward reduced the tenant's rental to the minimum level. The master does not make as much money as he would have liked. Neither does he lose any money because he has the minimum he expected to receive.

Scene 3: The steward gets unexpected praise

The master has his honour restored through receiving a good report of the steward. It implies that he is a good and honourable man, for the action of the man he has sacked has cast him in a good light. His tenants praise him for his generosity, so his stock rises.

Word will get around about the generous discounts which have been handed out. Everyone will want to be a tenant of this master! He wonders what to do. He can call the tenants back and tell them it was a big mistake, that the steward had been sacked and was acting without his authority. Or he can say nothing, accept the praise and allow the steward to have his honour restored too. He takes the second course of action, because he is a generous man. Generosity is a very important quality of Middle Eastern noblemen. There is nothing worse than having a reputation for being a miser.

Very pleased now that his reputation is restored, the master commends the steward. The nobleman is big-hearted, benevolent and even quite amused about the shrewd and audacious action which his former employee has taken. "Shrewd" is the same word as "wisdom, common sense, practical intelligence" (the Hebrew word is *sekhel*). The Jews would have said that the steward had lots of *sekhel*. The Old Testament definition of wisdom is "an instinct for self-preservation". Jesus commends this steward for being shrewd. In the same way that the steward's negligence reflected badly on the master, his cleverness is a compliment to him. The steward is therefore commended for his prudence, not for any fraud. His prudence is that he put his future before his present.

Western Christians are very reluctant to use a slightly shady character like this steward as a role model. We question how Jesus can invent such a man as the hero of one of his parables. But an Oriental boss is often delighted when an employee is clever enough to outwit him! It is a kind of compliment for the decision to employ him in the first place. A peasant at the bottom of the economic ladder in the Middle East, however, finds a parable like this pure delight. They love the kind of story where some David kills a Goliath. It is the same when we in the West heap praise on scoundrels like Robin Hood, who robbed the rich to give to the poor.

THEMES OF THE PARABLE

The parable ends with Jesus' comments about money. What lessons can we learn from this difficult parable?

First, we see that the steward was shrewd, clever, audacious and wise in the self-preservation sense but not dishonest. He was also negligent and wasteful in managing his master's properties. However, once caught, his actions were seen as prudent. He does something which restores both his and his master's reputations. Jesus commends his action for its prudence, not for fraud. The steward put his future before his present. He sacrificed his present to secure a welcome for his future. This is what Jesus is commending.

Second, Jesus makes a number of comments about the use of money. He commends the steward's action and points to him as an example of using money prudently in a crisis. In effect he is telling the disciples: "You, too, are going to be in a crisis, under pressure, so you need to think quick and like this steward learn how to use unrighteous money wisely." He is telling the disciples to use their money to "gain friends for yourselves so that when it is gone, you will be welcomed into eternal dwellings." Jesus clearly has the future in mind. This is a parable about using the money entrusted to us to invest for our eternal future. This is genuine long term investment. This is in contrast to the Rich Man in the next story who uses his money for his earthly comforts but neglected to secure his "eternal dwellings."

Third, Jesus says we need to be faithful with our money before we can be entrusted with "real riches." He is talking about treasures in heaven. He is saying that if we are not trustworthy in handling worldly wealth, we will not be trusted with "real riches." A problem with Christians in the West is that we have separated the "sacred" from the "secular" and tend to disregard the connection between what we do with money and the ministry God has entrusted to us. We are stewards of his treasures. When we handle money wisely, he will entrust us with "real riches." Jesus goes on to say that we need to be faithful with other people's money "otherwise who will give you property of your own?" (vs. 12)

Finally, Jesus teaches that we cannot serve two masters - God and money (vs. 13). In some churches today, it is actually preached that you can serve God and money and, in fact, the more you serve God the more prosperous you will become! This kind of prosperity teaching sits uncomfortably with the words of Jesus here. The Pharisees obviously thought you could serve God and money because they sneered at Jesus' teaching. They believed the rich stood a better chance of entering the kingdom because only the rich could offer to pay for the sacrifices, the tithes and keep all the commandments of the Law. The Pharisees were the "prosperity" teachers of their day.

Jesus' teachings about the Law
Sandwiched between the two "money parables" Luke has a selection of the sayings of Jesus. Most commentators consider these verses (v15 - 18) as disconnected remarks placed there by

Luke. However, when understood in their context, we can see them as Jesus' response to the Pharisees' reaction to his parable and teaching. They were "sneering at him" (v14) literally, "they were turning their noses up at him." The Law and the Prophets are mentioned twice (v16 and v31) suggesting that we should see this section as connected to the two stories.

Jesus' statement that the Law (the five books of Moses or the Torah) and the Prophets were preached until John the Baptist must have been difficult for the Pharisees to accept. Since then, the good news of the kingdom has been preached by Jesus. He does not mean that the Law and the Prophets are now void. To prevent this possible misunderstanding, he says that "it is easier for heaven and earth to disappear than for the least stroke of a pen to drop out of the Law." God's standard and just requirements as stated in the Law and the Prophets remain eternally true. However, the good news is that rather than relying on ourselves to meet these demanding standards, we now depend on the grace and the mercy of God to be accepted by him. The poor who cannot afford to keep all the commandments of the Law have the most to gain from this and that is why everyone is "forcing his way into the kingdom."

And then Jesus says something about divorce. This is not primarily a teaching on divorce. We would have to go elsewhere in Scripture for that. Rather, it is an example demonstrating that the Law and the Prophets continue to have authoritative force. The Pharisees have been selective about the parts of the Law which they are comfortable to observe. But the Law regarding money and divorce were interpreted more loosely for their convenience. They are warned that they cannot use their position to interpret the Law in an arbitrary manner.

After these comments, specifically directed at the Pharisees, Jesus then tells the story of the Rich Man and Lazarus to further underline the fact that the Law and the Prophets had strong teachings about how they should live and their attitudes to wealth and the poor. But the Pharisees conveniently ignore these. They pay tithes of little things like kitchen herbs and observe the details of other oral laws but neglect the heart of the Law, which is mercy.

8

THE RICH MAN AND LAZARUS
Luke 16:19-31

It was a great life! One long party in the huge, luxurious house he owned. Everything he could see, touch, eat and wear was the very best his vast wealth could buy. He did not have to worry about a thing - not like that beggar covered in horrible sores who sprawled outside his gate each day from morning till evening. It was just one of those things. Some are born to live that way, so there was no use helping the likes of him. Anyway, the money was needed for more important things - like this evening's feast ...

This parable has given scholars many problems over the years as they have struggled to understand its meaning. One problem is that one of the two key characters is actually named - Lazarus. In one of the older versions, the rich man is called Nineve. So scholars have wondered if this was just a story or an actual situation Jesus picked out and used to tell a story. There are, however, important reasons why Jesus should name the poor man Lazarus and we will come to this shortly.

A second problem is that a superficial reading of this parable suggests that its message is that the rich in this world will end up in hell, while the poor will go to heaven. But is this true? Is it consistent with the teachings of Jesus? Does the parable mean that those who experience hell now will enjoy heaven later and vice-versa? If it does, then many Christians will be in trouble. For, like it or not, we are all rich by the standards of the world. On this basis the rich are all destined for hell and the poor for heaven. We know that this is not what the Bible teaches because there are "bad" poor men as well as "good" rich men. So we need to look more carefully at what Jesus is saying here.

It should also be noted that Jesus uses a rich man in several of his stories. The father in the Lost Sons is a rich man and there is a rich man in the Lost Sheep, the Unrighteous Steward and the parable of the Talents. Zacchaeus was a rich man. Of these, only in the parable of the Rich Man and Lazarus and the story of Zacchaeus do riches come in for negative comment. In the other parables, Jesus does not comment about wealth. But he does in his other teachings with strong warnings, such as: "It is harder for a rich man to enter the kingdom than for a camel to go through the eye of a needle."

A third difficulty with this parable is that this is the only time Jesus describes "heaven" and "Hades." The question is, can we draw anything factual about these two places from this parable? Is hell a place of continuous fire? Will those in hell be conscious of their suffering? Is hell eternal torment or annihilation? An ongoing debate seeks to eliminate hell from the agenda, so can this parable be used to derive factual information about heaven and hell or are these places used as a convenient backdrop to the story? Will those in heaven and hell be able to communicate with each other? If this parable is factual, then this appears to be possible. We need to grapple with the various layers of difficulties that this parable raises.

This parable can be divided into three scenes.

Scene 1: Rich man and poor man - present state

Everything about the rich man was luxurious, his home, the food he consumed in vast quantities - and the quality of his clothes. His favourite colour was purple. Jesus tells us here that this man was wearing the kind of purple cloth robe normally worn by royalty. The fine linen he also wore was the high quality Egyptian cotton designer underwear that only the rich could afford.

Living in splendour every day meant that life for him was one feast after another. This man was just spending his vast amount of money on indulging himself without a thought for anyone else. He is also independent of God. Jesus wants us to hear his condemnation of and judgement upon this man. If people later on did give him the name Nineve, it echoes God's judgement upon the rich city of Ninevah during Old Testament times.

In direct contrast to the rich man is the desperate plight of the poor man. He lives in absolute squalor. Unlike the rich man, he has a name, Lazaros - La'azar, the Hebrew for *El Azar* which means "He whom God helps." That is the first hint as to why Jesus gives him this name. He wants his listeners to know that Lazarus is a pious poor man in this story. This is in stark contrast to the prevailing attitude of his day where the rich are regarded as righteous and destined for the kingdom, whereas the poor are not.

The poor man's piety is one of the reasons why he is the only one to be named by Jesus in this parable. He was in such a bad physical state that every day he was carried to the rich man's gate by friends or relatives. Every journey there is a venture of faith, because he does not know that he will get food there. Beggars being carried to a good place to beg for alms are daily scenes repeated in many countries of the East to this day. This is why this man is a son of Abraham because Abraham had also set out on a journey of faith. It is also why Abraham comes into the story later on. Lazarus is given his name to help us understand that he is a recipient of God's grace and help. He is righteous and pious, but poor - so poor that he has to throw himself on God's mercy every day he goes out. The poor have God on their side - only he will defend them. This is why Jesus said, "Blessed are you who are poor, for yours is the kingdom of God" (Lk. 6:20). But the rich, who think they have it all and feel they are secure, will not see the Kingdom.

Another reason why I believe Jesus named the poor man *El Azar* (Lazarus) is that it is the same name as Abraham's servant, Eliezar. So Jewish listeners of the parable would make that connection.

A third reason for the name in the parable is that Jesus is alluding to the other Lazarus whom everyone knew was raised from the dead, but whose resurrection failed to convert the Jewish leaders (Jn. 11:1-12:19). Use of the name Lazarus here would add to Jesus' punch line in verse 31: "... they will not be convinced even if someone rises from the dead."

Lazarus was left each day at the magnificent gate to the rich man's house. Jesus wanted his hearers to know that Lazarus was a familiar figure there and would have been noticed by the rich man every time he went in and out of his house. So it is implied that the rich man had countless opportunities to show mercy and help Lazarus. But the crux of the story is that he ignored the poor man, for all he was concerned about was indulging himself.

Covered with sores, Lazarus was ceremonially unclean according to Jewish laws on skin diseases. Only the dogs paid any attention to him - by licking him. That is unusual, for dogs in the Middle East are not household pets but wild dogs - ugly, mean-looking mongrels full of sores themselves. Yet in contrast to the rich man, these dogs have got so used to seeing Lazarus at the gate under the baking sun every day, became so friendly that they would lick and soothe his sores. Jesus is blatantly saying that the rich man was worse than his own dogs who at least showed some compassion for Lazarus! The insult is intended here.

Lazarus longed "to eat what fell from the rich man's table." This was not just breadcrumbs, but scraps of food, including meat on bones, which were thrown from the table for the dogs to clear up. Middle Eastern dogs were refuse bins as well as guard dogs. It saved on the washing up! In the Middle East, bread was used in two ways at meals. It would be broken into small pieces and used to dip into bowls to pick up meat and vegetables, acting a little like our forks and knives. Bread was also used to wipe the fingers after the meal and this would also be thrown to the dogs for scavenging. Despite his desperate situation, Lazarus was even denied those crumbs from the rich man's table which were fit only for dogs.

Scene 2: Poor man and rich man - future destiny

Now the tables are turned! Lazarus goes from misery to a place of utter comfort, while the rich man goes from opulence to torment. When Lazarus died he was so poor that he could not afford a funeral and is described in the story as carried by angels to Abraham's side. This is very unusual Jewish language, because the only other dead people carried by angels in the Bible are

Moses and Elijah. To be at someone's side is a lovely picture of intimacy and security, like the child lying on his or her parents' lap. At the beginning of John's gospel Jesus is so described: "No one has ever seen God, but he who is at the Father's side has made him known." John is saying that no one has been as close to God the Father as our Lord Jesus. It also describes the proximity of a guest to the host at a banquet (Jn. 13:23) and this is implied here.

Lazarus has left his poor state on earth for a banquet in heaven! He feasts at the Messianic banquet for eternity, sitting at the table with Abraham. No longer does he have to look for scraps of food to live on. Nothing is said about where Abraham is, but being at "Abraham's side" suggests both being in Paradise and being present at the Messianic banquet (Mt. 8:11). It is very difficult to formulate a doctrine of heaven and hell, and purgatory, from this story. Roman Catholic teaching on purgatory is derived from this parable, but this was not intended by Jesus. It is there as a backcloth. Telling stories and jokes about heaven and hell is commonplace in the Middle East, so it would be wrong to make a doctrine out of the details here.

The rich man goes on enjoying his daily feasts on earth and probably does not even notice that Lazarus was not around any more. He eventually dies, but unlike Lazarus, he can afford a burial. A big elaborate funeral is implied by his vast wealth. The rich man failed to realise that it was not the farewell from this life but the welcome on the other side that was important. But he goes to Hades instead of Heaven. It is again difficult to pinpoint the precise state and location of Hades from the parable, and it is not intended that we should. It is part of the backdrop to the story. The word used by Jesus is Hades, not hell. According to Jewish teaching, Hades is the place where spirits of dead people are resting awaiting the Day of Judgement. It is not wholly a place of punishment, but this passage seems to indicate it includes one. In the end Hades itself will be thrown into the lake of fire (Rev. 20:13-15).

One of the richest men in the world used to live in Guildford. His name was Paul Getty and he made his fortune from oil. But he became a pauper - one minute after he died. As someone has said, death duties everywhere are 100%. You leave everything behind. The rich man too, became a pauper after he died.

On his arrival at Hades, the rich man opens his eyes to see Abraham in the distance and, to his surprise, Lazarus with him. Listeners to this parable would have immediately reacted at this, exclaiming: "That's all wrong!" Jesus makes a shocking statement by saying the rich man went to Hades. It was widely thought that the rich would be saved, because only they could afford to keep the commandments of the Law. The poor did not stand a chance of keeping all the commandments. But this is the thrust of the story: Jesus is attacking this widely held belief that only the rich can be saved. He turned things upside down with this parable. The poor man goes to heaven. The rich man goes to Hades. The rich man is now living in agony and torment in contrast to Lazarus. It may be difficult for people in the West to get the full impact of this parable, because we do not have the culture to understand it. It is perhaps better understood in a country like India, where the rich are very rich and the poor desperately poor, and where the perception is that the rich are superior and are higher up in the re-incarnation cycle.

Jesus may also be taking a swipe at any Sadducees among his listeners by pointing to a physical resurrection - something which they did not believe in. But the most important thing he wants to get across at this stage of the story is that the rich may not always be saved and go to heaven.

The rich man is separated by an unbridgeable gulf between him and Abraham and the saints. He is also separated by an unbridgeable gulf with the living. He cannot communicate with those still alive on earth to warn them against suffering a similar fate to himself. And he cannot expect any mercy because he had failed to show mercy to Lazarus. The fortunes and eternal destinies of these two men had been reversed.

Jesus is giving a very clear "Wealth Warning": "Don't let your riches destroy you! Don't spend your wealth selfishly so that your heart is hardened and you become indifferent towards the poor."

Scene 3: Talks between the rich man and Abraham

In the first of three conversations, the rich man instructs Abraham: "... send Lazarus ..." But he is not exactly in a position to instruct Abraham! This is the kind of Middle Eastern irony Jesus' audience would be expected to laugh at. Jewish humour is often what is called "black humour"- seeing the funny side of adversity. This is what we have here. This rich man is so used to being wealthy and bossy, giving orders to everybody else, having his own way, that even when he is down in Hades he is so thick that he thinks he can give orders to Abraham. The listeners would have smiled at this bit of story telling.

In Hades, the rich man still thinks of Lazarus as a good-for-nothing; fit only to be a servant. He is totally unrepentant, still concerned only about himself. The only thing he cares about is something to quench his thirst in the fires of Hades. He calls Lazarus by name, revealing that he knows him by sight and plight (yet never did anything to help him.) He precedes his instruction to Abraham with a cry for mercy - but how could he expect mercy when he had failed to show any to Lazarus in his earthly "hell"? It is too late. Before he died, the rich man had servants. Now he is a beggar asking for water. By contrast, Lazarus the former beggar now has angels as his servants. The roles have been reversed.

Here then is the pride of the wealthy coming to the fore. Rich people think there is nothing that money cannot buy - including people and influence. Wealth buys a lifestyle and attitude that believes that one can get one's own way all the time. The rich man of this parable certainly believed that. He has a real attitude problem, which is why he is where he is - in Hades.

The rich man's arrogance in giving orders to Abraham, the spiritual father of Israel and one looked upon as having authority and influence with God (see Lk. 3:8) is dealt with in Abraham's reply. He calls the rich man "child" - a term of endearment, an acknowledgement of their human relationship. And in this gentleness we are to see the appeal of Jesus to the self-righteous people around him. But this kinship does not entitle him to any

117

favours. Abraham reminds him that he received "good things" during his lifetime - he literally enjoyed "the good life" but now that was over and he was condemned to pain and torment. Lazarus has had a bad life on earth, but is now being comforted in heaven.

Abraham tells the rich man that not only is help unavailable, but there is an eternal separation between them. It is an irrevocable judgement. Eternal destiny, once fixed at death, cannot be changed. That is the tough message. For his disciples, it should act as a solemn warning that we need to live our lives now in the context of eternity.

The rich man does not give up even when given this devastating news. Although he has resigned himself to his own fate, he now seeks to prevent his brothers from suffering the same agonies. He begs, rather than orders Abraham to send Lazarus as a messenger to the family home to warn them about Hades. The rich man still has not accepted the message that he has no rights whatsoever. He continues to behave like an arrogant rich man and the listeners would have smiled at this further touch of humour by Jesus.

The five brothers lived at home with their father, probably because the family estate has not been broken up yet. There are echoes of the parable of the Lost Sons here when, before the dividing up of the inheritance, all the family members were together (Lk. 15:11-12; cf 12:13).

Abraham's answer to the rich man's plea is that the brothers have access to Moses and the Prophets - "Let them hear them." These men can go to the synagogue, hear the Scripture readings and respond to the message in them. They have got enough messengers - they do not need another one.

The rich man continues to argue. He knows that his family has never taken any notice of what the Law and the Prophets say - it needed something more dramatic for them to take the message seriously. "if someone (raised) from the dead goes to them, they will repent." This is typical of the persistence of rich men, especially in the East. They try instructions and bullying first, then if they do not get their way they will try pleading. If that does not work they resort to arguing and reasoning until they get their own way. The wealthy will not take "No" for an answer - there has got to be a way. All else having failed, the rich man of the parable asks for a miracle - a supernatural manifestation.

Abraham refuses this request, because if they will not listen to the Law and Prophets they will not believe it if someone rises from the dead. In this Jesus is looking ahead to his resurrection when, even with such evidence, the Jews would still not believe. Miracles will not convince morally blind and unrepentant hearts. The Jews had already witnessed the resurrection of the other Lazarus from the grave and did not believe and repent. Another greater resurrection, of Jesus himself, would take place but they would still remain unconvinced.

THEMES OF THE PARABLE
What can we learn from this parable?

First, it is faith that gets a person to heaven. Lazarus - "he whom God helps" is a true son of Abraham, a son of faith. He is righteous and pious, as his name implies. The dual meaning in this story is that the other Lazarus who was raised from the dead was known to everyone and those who had ears to hear among Jesus' listeners would have made that connection. Lazarus went to heaven because of his faith as a son of Abraham, not because of his economic poverty. There is no merit in poverty in itself.

Second, it is wrong for a person to trust in riches to save him. The rich man of this story tried this. He lived in self-centred luxury and did not show compassion for the poor. There is nothing basically wrong with wealth - it is the misuse and abuse of it that Jesus condemns. Wealth should be used to show mercy. We have all been warned: we could end up like the rich man of this parable unless we repent and change our lives.

Third, the listeners of the parable were meant to be one of the five brothers, so they have to put themselves in the shoes of one of these men. How would they react to this story? Would they repent if someone rose from the dead? Would they change your lifestyle? Would they change their attitude to wealth and material possessions?

Fourth, the parable speaks about the use of money. Jesus attacks the popular concept that only the rich will be saved. That is a real shock for the listeners. Elsewhere in the Bible he says it is harder for a rich man to enter the Kingdom of God than for a camel to go through the eye of a needle. It is a warning that "the good life" on earth can lead to agony and torment in hell for eternity. Jesus had far more to say about the use of money than immorality. Jesus said, if you have not been faithful in the use of unrighteous money, how can anyone entrust you with the true riches? This rich man did not know how to handle the wealth that God had given him. Jesus is not saying here that wealth is inherently wrong. Faith means showing mercy in being generous and compassionate with the wealth God has given you.

Fifth, miracles alone will not lead people to repentance. Jesus predicts his resurrection and also predicts that the Jews will still not believe in him despite the miracle. People follow after signs, wonders, healings, but they do not lead to repentance.

Sixth, we have a glimpse of heaven and Hades in this story. Lazarus lying by Abraham's side is an image of heaven. But the story does not give us details about either. What we learn about both places can be summarised as follows:

1. Jesus tells us that both places exist and, for some, death will be better, for others it will be worse. *How* we live now determines *where* we will live in the future.

2. Death is not the end of human consciousness. Hades is described as a place of agony and torment and heaven as a place of comfort.

3. Once there our eternal destinies are fixed. There are unbridgeable gulfs between heaven, Hades and earth. It is too late for remorse and regrets.

All these details add up to an extremely uncomfortable, soul-searching parable!

Comparison with the Parable of the Prudent Steward

Luke has put these two stories together in order to compare and contrast them. There are similarities in their contents and message. Here are some of them:

Both stories begin with the phrase "There was a rich man..." In the first, the rich man is the master and he is contrasted with the steward. But in the story, the principal actor is the steward. In the second, it is the rich man who is contrasted with Lazarus, but the principal character in the story is the rich man. So the intention is that we should compare the actions of the steward with that of the rich man in the second story.

The steward was called to give an account by his master. Similarly the rich man also had to give an account. But this does not happen until he was dead and in Hades. Both experienced unexpected tragedies - the steward with dismissal; the rich man with death. The steward had a comfortable life but was threatened with future poverty as a result of his negligence. The rich man was rich but was reduced to poverty at his death because of his indifference.

The steward used his position and wealth to win friends and secure a welcome for his future. The rich man did not. He lived selfishly and put his present well being before his future destiny. The steward is praised for his prudence whilst the rich man is judged for his selfish living and lack of concern for others.

9

THE JUDGE AND THE WIDOW
Luke 18:1-8

He knew from the moment he woke up that a certain thing would happen that day in court. That woman would be there. And she would be interrupting the cases he was hearing by shouting: "Grant me justice!" She would be back tomorrow and the next day and the day after that - same time, same place, yelling for the same thing. She was getting on his nerves - and even invading his dreams. He had woken up more than once in cold sweat believing wildly for a few moments that he had had another confrontation with this wretched widow. If this went on much longer he would end up with a nervous breakdown. There was only one way of keeping his sanity - give her what she is asking for ...

This is one of the few parables about prayer that Jesus told his disciples. It is unusual in that, with this and the parable of the Pharisee and the Tax Collector, Luke tells us the purpose of these stories at the beginning. He says that they are to show the disciples that they ought to pray at all times and not lose heart. None of the other parables tell us their meaning at the beginning. They leave it to the listeners to work it out at the end.

The parable of the Judge and the Widow is a very simple story about persistence in prayer. But do not be deceived. Jesus uses the story to address some very complex issues. For instance, there is the issue of God's righteousness and justice. How can we say God is just and all-powerful when there is so much injustice in the world? God does not seem to hear us when we cry out to him against suffering and injustice. Here Jesus deals, at least in part, with this issue. It is therefore an important parable.

The clearest instructions in the Bible about the appointment of judges are in 2 Chronicles 19:4-7. There King Jehoshaphat is given instructions by the Lord: "He appointed judges in the land, in each of the fortified cities of Judah. He told them, 'Consider carefully what you do, because you are not judging for man but for the Lord, who is with you whenever you give a verdict. Now let the fear of the Lord be upon you. Judge carefully, for with the Lord our God, there is no injustice or partiality or bribery."

The judges were appointed to pass judgement on ordinary issues brought by people to the city gate. They were instructed to judge righteously, impartially and without demanding or accepting bribes. They were to judge in the fear of the Lord. There were strong and clear instructions laid down, but sadly these were not always heeded and corruption was rampant in the judiciary. This corruption became a standing joke in Israel during Old Testament times. There was so much of it that God had to send prophet after prophet to speak against the injustices of the judges.

Amos was one of those prophets: "For three sins of Israel, even for four, I will not turn back my wrath. They sell the righteous for silver, and the needy for a pair of sandals. They trample upon the heads of the poor ... and deny justice to the oppressed" (Amos 2:6-7). Further on, the prophet takes up the same theme: "You hate the one who reproves in court and despise him who tells the truth. You trample on the poor and force him to give you grain ... You oppress the righteous and take bribes and you deprive the poor of justice in the courts" (Amos 5:10-12).

It is a vivid picture of the corruption in the judicial system of the day - corruption which continued into New Testament times. The Jews of the day had a nickname for rotten judges that is a play on words. Instead of calling them by their full title, *Dayyaney Gezeroth,* meaning "Judges of Prohibition," they are mischievously called, *Dayyaney Gezeloth,* meaning "Robber judges"! This parable is Jesus' commentary on the corrupt judiciary system of the day. The poor were defenceless and could expect little justice.

There are three scenes to this parable, with one final application.

Scene 1: Powerful judge
"In a certain town there was a judge who neither feared God nor had respect for people.." The judge is a symbol of authority and

unlimited power. His judgements were final. Jesus paints the picture of a man who has no time for God and his ways. This, as we have seen, is contrary to Jehoshaphat's instructions to the judges to fear God and exercise justice in that fear because God would judge the judges one day. This judge, however, does not respect God's laws. There was no point appealing to God's sense of justice with this man. It would be a waste of time.

This judge is callous, hard-hearted and arrogant. Not only does he have no fear of God, he has no respect for people either. The word "respect" in Greek can be translated "shame". In other words, he is not ashamed before people. The Oriental culture is based on shame and "face-saving" as we have seen from the parable of the Friend at Midnight. Face is everything. To lose face means to lose honour and therefore to be shamed. Oriental parents do not appeal to a child's sense of right and wrong by saying: "Don't do that because that's wrong." Instead, they would say, "Don't do that because it's shameful." To be shamed before people is a serious matter of one's honour. The prospect of being publicly shamed is a strong deterrent against wrong action. One of the sharpest criticisms one can make about any person is to say: "He feels no shame."

Not only does this judge lack a fear of God and a sense of shame, he has no honour whatsoever. He is thick-skinned and mercenary. He is hurting a destitute widow. At least he should feel ashamed of that, but he is not. "Ashamed" here is exactly the same word used to describe the rebellious tenants in Luke 20:13. The master sends his servants to the tenants, but these messengers are ignored. He finally sends his beloved son: "Perhaps they will respect him." In other words: "Maybe they will feel shamed before him." But they did not. They killed him instead.

There was no way of getting through to this judge except through bribery. In Oriental cultures, procrastinations and delays are often signals that a bribe is required. This was, and continues to be, common practice in many countries.

Scene 2: A powerless widow

A widow in the judge's town kept coming to him and pleading: "Grant me justice." It is interesting that Jesus chose a widow for his story, because such a person is a symbol of the innocent, the powerless, the oppressed and the weak in society. She was a total contrast to the judge. She had no one to defend her rights and interests.

This is what the prophet Isaiah has to say about justice and how to treat people like her: "Stop doing wrong, learn to do right! Seek justice, encourage the oppressed. Defend the cause of the fatherless, plead the case of the widow" (Is. 1:16-17). Jeremiah echoes this. "This is what the Lord says: Do what is just and right. Rescue from the hand of the oppressor the one who has been robbed. Do no wrong or violence to the alien, the fatherless and the widow, and do not shed innocent blood" (Jer. 22:3).

On the basis of these Scriptures, Jewish law required that all law suits or cases relating to orphans should always be heard first. Next in order of priority in the law courts were all cases relating to widows. God laid down tremendously good laws in the Old Testament. They gave this woman a legitimate right to demand that her case be heard by the judge. The problem was that because he neither feared God nor had any sense of shame towards people, he refused to hear the case. This woman is too weak to compel and too poor to buy justice. She has no influential connections, so there is no one to promote her cause. Justice in those days was based on a "who you know" basis.

What kind of problem did this destitute widow have? It certainly has something to do with money. According to Jewish law, a single qualified scholar could sit and make judgement in money cases. More complex cases were decided by at least two or three judges. She was not after revenge, but was asking to be vindicated - "Grant me justice against my adversary." Her request is for legal protection from her opponent. She does not want vengeance, only justice for herself.

Widows seem to attract the vultures. It is interesting that prior to this parable, Jesus had mentioned that vultures will gather

126

where there is a dead body (Lk. 17:37). Whether the mention of vultures led him to think about this widow is not made known. Widows then, as now, are soft targets for the unscrupulous. They are easily exploited and are often the ones to suffer when pension funds go bankrupt. This is why God laid down laws to protect them. This widow certainly needed protection from someone who was exploiting her. So she cries out for justice. Jeremias suggests that a debt, pledge or something of that nature was being kept from her.

There are several assumptions that are made in this story. The first is that the widow is right. The second is that the judge is corrupt. He does not want to save her. He will not give her a minute of his time unless, perhaps, she can offer him a bribe. Third, the widow's opponent is obviously someone influential who, perhaps, is persuading the judge not to hear the case.

An Oriental listener would have realised that the story has a very unusual feature. Women do not normally go to court in the Middle East. It is usually the men who do so. This indicates that she was entirely alone. Normally it is the son who fights the case on his mother's behalf. But Jesus deliberately paints the story of this poor, defenceless woman who is totally alone and has to go to court herself.

If you were a man and went to court as this woman did and started to badger the judge, you would be in danger of being arrested and thrown into jail. But a woman in an Oriental society can get away with this kind of disruptive behaviour. So although a woman is regarded generally as powerless, they are also respected and honoured. Men may be mistreated in public, but not women. This woman can scream at the judge and get away with it. A man cannot. So despite her desperate situation, she does have certain things in her favour.

A 19th century story told by Kenneth Bailey tells of an incident in the ancient city of Nisibis in Mesopotamia where, in the court of justice, sat the *kadi* (judge), half-buried in cushions listening to cases. During this time, a woman on the fringes of the crowd kept on interrupting the proceedings by crying out for justice.

She was told sternly to be silent, but continued to come every day and said she would carry on doing so "until the *kadi* hears me." Eventually, at the end of one case, the judge impatiently demanded: "What does that woman want?" He was told that her only son had been forcibly recruited into the army and she was left alone and could not till her piece of land. Yet she had been forced to pay tax when, in fact, as a lone widow she was legally exempt. After asking a few questions, the judge said: "Let her be exempt." Her perseverance was rewarded. If she had had the money to bribe a clerk, she might have been excused long before.

Scene 3: Persistent widow

In Jesus' parable, the widow's persistence and her daily yelling for justice at the city gate eventually penetrates the hard-hearted judge's defences. Even at night, long after the daily court sessions are over, her voice echoes in his brain. It causes him to do a lot of hard thinking. "But finally he said to himself, 'Even though I do not fear God or care about men, yet because this widow keeps bothering me, I will see that she gets justice, so that she won't wear me out ...'"

"Wear me out" is a telling phrase. It comes from boxing and is used when a man hits his opponent under the eye. Not that the judge expects this woman to become violent (she would be evicted if she did) but as the Arabic translations put it, "Lest she comes and gives me a headache!" This shows how much the woman's persistence has irked the judge.

We in the West tend to have a reverse sense of pride and integrity. We come and ask somebody for something once and may stretch to asking a second time. But we would be too embarrassed to ask a third time. There is generally no such sense of shame in the Middle East about continually asking for something - day after day after day. The Oriental culture permits you to go on asking until you get it.

The judge believes this woman will never give up until she gets what she wants. The Greek phrase for her continual coming is strong, implying that the woman had the will to go on forever.

The confrontation between widow and judge is akin to a war of attrition. It is a case of who is going to be worn out first.

Jesus is saying that if the needs of this widow are being met, how much more will the needs of the disciples who petition a loving heavenly Father rather than an unrighteous judge. In the same way that the widow persevered, we need to keep on asking. If an unrighteous judge was willing in the end to meet her needs, to vindicate and bring justice to this helpless widow, how much more will your loving heavenly Father vindicate you when you plead with him in prayer.

Jesus wants his listeners to understand the contrast between the widow and the disciples. The widow had her legal rights violated and one day the same will happen to the disciples too. The widow was up against the authorities and she was fearful; the disciples will be hauled up before authorities, kings and princes because of their witness and they too, will be fearful. Like the widow, the disciples will also be in situations where they will be alone and defenceless. The widow had no influence socially and politically, nor had she the money to get herself out of trouble. The disciples will also find themselves in similar situations. Therefore the disciples are to take heart from the example of this woman. She petitioned day after day and was finally vindicated. The disciples, too, will be finally vindicated if they persevere.

Jesus' application

Jesus now takes up the story and applies it to the issue of God's apparent slowness at answering prayers. He starts by saying, "Listen to what the unjust judge says. And will not God bring about justice for his chosen ones, who cry out to him day and night? Will he keep putting them off? I tell you, he will see that they get justice, and quickly. However, when the Son of Man comes, will he find faith (or faithfulness) on the earth?"

The judge said: "I will see that she gets justice ..." Jesus assures his disciples by saying "he will see that they get justice..." A key word in this parable is "justice," which can also mean vindication or judgement. In other words, when God brings justice for the righteous, He will also have to bring his judgement with him. We cannot have one without the other. This is why God is sometimes slow to act on the prayers of his people. If God was to bring justice now he would have to judge us now as well. Do we really want his judgement now?

There is a marvellous story told by the rabbis of a king who wondered where to station his troops. In the end he decided to send them some distance from the capital so that, if civil disobedience broke out it would take time to bring them in. That would give the rebels the opportunity to come to their senses. So it was argued, "God keeps his wrath at a distance in order to give Israel time to repent." This is the picture we have in these verses. God delays, puts his anger at a distance to give us time to come to our senses and repent. He is slow in his anger with us.

Jesus then says that his chosen ones will "get justice, and quickly" (vs. 8). God assures us that he will bring justice and when it comes, it will be swift. His delay should not be seen as neglect but rather as an expression of his mercy. We want justice, but we do not want his judgement. Jesus uses this parable to show why at times God's justice seems to be delayed. It is so that we will have time to repent. This is the kind of tension we have all the time. On the one hand, we want God to answer us quickly, but on the other, we want him to delay his wrath.

Jesus then concludes with these words: "When the Son of Man comes, will he find faith on the earth?"(vs. 8) Someone, either Jesus himself or Luke, is very nervous about the less-than-perfect disciples around him. He is not sure that these disciples are going to endure, to persevere like the widow in the parable did. He is fearful that his disciples will fail to pray, lose heart and in the end lose faith. The parable is seeking to teach us that it is vitally important to learn how to persevere in prayer.

THEMES OF THE PARABLE
What can we learn from this story?

First, Jesus instructs us that we need to learn how to pray in situations where there is hopelessness, helplessness and fear. We are encouraged to keep on storming the gates of heaven with our petitions - "Lord, it's me again."

Second, we can come with more confidence than this widow because we pray to a loving heavenly Father, not to an unrighteous judge. If a corrupt judge finally gives in to the widow's pestering, how much more will God, who is just, respond to his chosen people's continual prayers.

Third, God will hear our prayers for justice, but we need to understand that he does put his anger aside to hear our prayers. As the Book of Revelation tells us, God's wrath is ready and waiting to be poured out, but it is held back so that he can hear the prayers of his faithful ones. In a sense it is us, his praying community on earth, who are holding back this wrath.

Fourth, if God delays his justice, it is an indication of his mercy. But he will finally bring vindication, so do not lose heart in prayer. This will be hard, which is why Jesus is encouraging his disciples with these words at the end of the parable.

Fifth, the widow is used as an example of faithful prayer. Most of us, especially men, struggle with prayer. We find it even harder to keep on praying over an issue. Jesus holds up this widow as a model of perseverance in prayer.

10

THE TALENTS
Luke 19:19-27

Word rapidly spread. It reached the servants' ears: "The master is on his way back!" The head servant beamed. He looked forward to the inevitable interview with his boss in the next day or so, for he had done well during the latter's absence. In fact, he had become a real entrepreneur with the money given to him. The deputy head servant was also pleased at the prospect of seeing his boss again. He could show a healthy profit from the trading he had done. But one servant looked absolutely terrified. Now he wished he had done something useful with the money he had been given ...

The rise of what has been called "prosperity teaching" derived from this parable has caused me to take a long look at this story. If we read this parable through Western capitalist eyes it appears to be an account of two successful and one failed businessman. Rewards were promised to those who were successful. The bigger the profits, the more they would be rewarded, or so it seems. In today's world of rampant materialism it is all too easy to read it through these tinted glasses.

This kind of interpretation is given in a number of Christian books: "God wants you to be rich and successful!" is the message. The reason we do not have a swimming pool in our garden, own a boat or drive a Rolls Royce, we are told, is because we do not have the faith. We have what some writers call a "bicycle faith." It means that if you have faith only for a bicycle, that is what you will get. But if you have faith for a Rolls Royce, you will have one. Advocates of this kind of teaching point to the two servants becoming accomplished businessmen and their successful enterprises bringing rich rewards for them.

We need, however, to question this kind of interpretation: Is Jesus really advocating material success and profits? Is this interpretation consistent with the rest of his teaching and lifestyle? The disciples certainly would not have understood this parable in such crude materialistic terms. They all died poor, after all, as did Jesus!

Well, we will need to look again at the Oriental background and the context in order to understand this story correctly. This parable in Luke's gospel follows Jesus' encounter with Zacchaeus, the tax collector who repented of the misuse of wealth and found salvation through God's Son. While still with Zacchaeus, Jesus began to tell his disciples this parable "because he was near Jerusalem." The crowd was following him into Jerusalem, expecting him to lead a popular uprising to overthrow the Romans and bring in the kingdom of God right away. Because of this, says Luke, Jesus told the parable of the Talents. This, then, is the proper context to understand this story.

The parable was used by Jesus to tell his disciples about *when* the Kingdom was coming (Lk. 19:11). It was told during the last week of Jesus' life on earth. He is going to Jerusalem to face the Cross, so he wants his disciples to know when to expect the coming of the Kingdom of God. And he does so in a classical style by telling this story about a nobleman getting ready to go off to a distant land to receive a kingdom or throne and then return.

Scene 1: Nobleman's departure

This story has an authentic background. The kings of Israel from Herod onwards had to go to Rome to gain permission from Caesar to rule as king. The one closest to the time of Jesus was Archelaus, son of Herod the Great. After his father's death in 4 BC, Archelaus went to Rome for confirmation as king. But he was so disliked in Israel that a deputation of fifty Jews successfully protested to Augustus with the result that the emperor gave Archelaus only half his father's kingdom. They did not want Archelaus to rule over them.

So the story, shrewdly set against the political scene of the day, would have been readily understood by Jesus' disciples. The nobleman has a right to become king, but has to go off to a distant country to receive that kingdom. Then he is going to return. That nobleman is a picture of Jesus himself. He too has to go to a "distant country" to receive the Kingdom in full. Then he will return.

The nobleman's bags are being packed ready for this vitally important journey. So he calls ten of his servants to tell them what to do while he is away. He gives each a *mina*, the equivalent of a hundred days' wages, and instructs them to trade with the money until he comes back. It is important to understand what the nobleman is seeking to do with his servants, because this is the key to the parable. He wants them to trade with the money openly and faithfully because he is definitely coming back

This leaves the servants with important choices to make. Are they going to be bold enough to trade publicly, like starting a carpet store in the centre of Jerusalem, or would it be too big a risk to do so? Then, as now in the Middle East and many parts of the world, the choices have to be made amidst a political tinderbox. If they did as the master said, all would be well for them if he did come back as king. But if he was to be overthrown, his loyal servants would be swiftly dealt with by his opponents.

Political instability and intrigues have often resulted in coups when the country's leader is away visiting another country. The heads of Commonwealth conferences during the 1960s and 70s were regular occasions for Prime Ministers of developing member countries in Africa, to lose their jobs in absentia. And those who had openly backed the deposed leader often lost their lives. It was a matter of life and death to be on the "winning" side.

The servants in the parable knew that their master had many enemies who did not want him as king. So his instruction meant a minefield of risks for them. The only assurance they have is his promise that he will be back and he has also given them some venture capital for the work he wants doing. How they act depends on what they think of their master, whether they believe he is coming back to rule. So this parable is not about material prosperity, but about how the disciples are to act while they wait for their coming king. It is about faithfulness, loyalty and courage, of nailing one's colours to the mast.

Imagine the last days of President Mobutu of Zaire, one of the most corrupt African regimes ever. He is preparing to leave the country and calls his officials together, telling them to continue to run his businesses whilst he is away. He assures them that he is coming back. His officials should be faithful in their duties and they should not be afraid to be seen carrying on their trading activities on his behalf. How many officials do you think will be bold enough to publicly run their businesses in his name? This is a similar situation here in this parable. Only those servants who trusted the nobleman and believed he was coming back would be loyal and faithful during his absence.

So hated is the nobleman by people in the country he sought to be king over that they tried to stop him being crowned. The force of this opposition is seen in the correct translation of Luke 19:14, "We don't want *this* to be our king." The word "man" is missing in the Greek, emphasising the contempt the people had for their would-be ruler. Jesus tells it like this to show how he will be rejected by the Jews and crucified.

Scene 2: Nobleman's return

To everyone's surprise, the nobleman is made king and returns. Most of his subjects had written him off and betted against his return. The story now takes on an air of expectancy.

After being crowned king, the nobleman returns as he has promised and sends for his servants to find out how business has gone, what they have gained by trading. He is not primarily interested in how much profit they have made, but how much trading they have done. "How regularly did you open the shop and how did you publicise the business? How boldly did you trade with the money I gave you?" Faithfulness to the master amidst the political turmoil, not profit, was what was all-important to him. But with the first two servants, faithfulness also resulted in fruitfulness and success in their ventures.

The first servant tells him that he has turned the master's *mina* into ten. That is a tremendous return on investment and brought due commendation for being faithful with what he had been given. And because he has acted faithfully with a small amount he is given more responsibility - authority over ten cities. It is hard to make a case for prosperity teaching from this because it is about being given added responsibility, not materialistic reward.

Similarly the next servant, who has turned his *mina* into five of them, is given the added responsibility of looking after five cities. He, too, has been bold and brave enough to trade openly and successfully for his master.

But the third servant has let the side down. He obviously had not expected the master to return, so he hid the money he was given. His excuse was that he was afraid of the master but, in reality, he was scared to take the risk of being identified too closely with the nobleman in case he did not return as king. He did not trust the master, so he tried to avoid ending up on the losing side. He kept his lamp under a bushel so no one was able to see it. His unfaithfulness made him into what he cowardly tried to avoid - a loser.

Scene 3: Nobleman's judgement

The nobleman-turned-king now passes judgement on two groups of people. The first is his cowardly servant and the second, his enemies who did not want him to be king.

The third servant said he put the money in a handkerchief "... because you are a hard man. You take out what you did not put in and reap what you did not sow." That was a strong accusation, especially coming from a servant. The master responded to this by telling the man: "I will judge you by your own words!" Even if it were true, why was not the money simply put in the bank? It is implied here that it did not matter how much profit was made on the investment, but as long as something had been made, the servant would have been regarded as good and faithful.

The servant has not even done this simple thing because he was afraid and ashamed to bear his master's name. In opening a bank account, he would have had to disclose whose money it was. This is further evidence that the parable is not just about success, but about loyalty and faithfulness.

If the slave's accusation is correct, he is condemned by his own words. He is even more condemned if his assessment of the master is wrong. It is very clear that Jesus is identifying himself with the nobleman, so this assessment is very wrong indeed.

The master orders the *mina* to be taken away by onlookers and given to the servant who has ten. They protest: "He's got a lot, so why give him more?" It is not fair when viewed in materialistic terms, but it is absolutely right when understood in terms of faithfulness, of standing up for him while he is away. The labourers in the vineyard received the same pay even though they did not work the same number of hours. That too sounds unfair, but these parables are not about reward. The crunch is that those who are faithful, loyal and take risks for the master will be given more responsibility. But those who are unfaithful will have what little they possess taken away from them.

Finally, there is judgement on his enemies, those who did not want the nobleman to rule over them. Imagine one of those deposed Commonwealth Prime Ministers staging a successful counter-coup. Woe betide those who had sought to overthrow him! This is the force of the concluding verse of this parable.

THEMES OF THE PARABLE
We can now summarise this interesting story:

First, it teaches us that the Kingdom of God will not be immediate. Jesus is going away for a time. He will receive the Kingdom and return - definitely! During this interregnum, he expects us to be faithful to him as we await the coming King. Jesus is departing and will not be appointed King until he returns. The people desperately wanted to make Jesus king when he made his triumphant entry into Jerusalem, but in telling this parable, he is saying that he cannot be truly made King until he has gone away and come back.

Second, the people he is to rule over will reject him and can expect judgement. This is a strong warning to the listeners who are hostile to Jesus.

Third, the parable tells us that a token gift of the Kingdom has been entrusted to men during this interregnum period. Before the nobleman went away, he gave a token gift to his servants. It represents a guarantee that Jesus is coming back. Our responsibility is to be faithful, not merely successful or highly profitable. The first servant made a ten-fold return on capital. The second a five-fold return. Both were commended by the master. If the third had made a two-fold return on capital, he too would have been commended for his faithfulness. The parable therefore encourages his disciples to unashamedly show that they belong to Jesus by trading in his name and be seen to be associated with him. They are to fly his flag high. They are to cast their lot with the "nobleman," Jesus, because he is coming back. It will be risky to remain loyal during his absence.

Matthew's version of the parable
There are some differences of emphases between Luke and Matthew's versions of this parable. Again this is determined by the context in which the parables are found.

The context in Matthew 25:14-30 is about the coming judgement. The previous chapter (verses 45-51), contains the parable of the unfaithful servant who did not know when the master was coming and could not care less. Judgement in the form of horrific death and being consigned to a place of torment was their "reward." This is followed in Matthew 25:1-13 by the Parable of the Ten Virgins, which emphasises being faithful and alert, waiting and being ready for the coming King. Next comes the parable of the Talents, followed by separation of the sheep and goats (25:31-33) and Jesus' teaching on faithfully serving him - "For I was hungry and you gave me ..." (25:34-46), a theme which also ends up in judgement for the unrighteous.

As well as the emphasis on judgement - "weeping and gnashing of teeth" (24:51; 25:30) and "the eternal fire prepared for the devil and his angels" (25:41) - there is also the theme of faithfulness. The loyal servants wait for their master to return so that they can serve him; the faithful virgins are ready for the bridegroom; the servants are faithful with their talents and the faithful disciples feed the hungry, clothe the naked and refresh the thirsty.

Above all, the Parable of the Talents is a call to be faithful and to remain loyal. This calls for courageous actions. The Kingdom has been entrusted to us and it is our responsibility to use its spiritual benefits faithfully until the Kingdom comes in fullness when Jesus returns as King.

Prosperity theology

The Parable of the Talents does not say anything about prosperity. A lot of exegesis from this parable by prosperity teachers has been made without regards to the context and background. Much of such teaching is inconsistent with the teaching and life of Jesus and the apostles. None of them were rich or "successful" materially.

While state churches, notably the Roman Catholic Church under emperor-like popes, became prosperous with acquisition of land and wealth in the hundreds of years after Christ's resurrection, modern prosperity teaching largely comes from affluent Western charismatic leaders. The only people who seem to benefit from this kind of teaching are the leaders themselves, not the ordinary members! Beware of leaders living lifestyles that are more affluent than those of the members of their congregations.

As the issue of this parable is not just about success but how faithful and fruitful we are while Jesus is away, how bold are we then in standing up for Jesus during the interregnum?

11

ZACCHAEUS
Luke 18:35-19:10

It was a carnival and a protest march all rolled into one. The excited crowd had gathered round their hero as he walked through the city, heading for the capital. And when he stopped and insisted on healing the blind man, their celebrations became noisier and wilder. They really believed this man was going to do what they had dreamed of for so long - lead an armed insurrection, throw out the hated occupiers and restore their country to its former glory. Their celebrations were brought to an abrupt halt just as they were leaving the city behind them. Their hero walked over to the first sycamore tree and started to talk to the little man sitting in its lower branches. Suddenly the mood changed ...

The story of Zacchaeus is not a parable because it was an incident that actually took place in the life of Jesus. Our Lord followed the tradition of the Old Testament prophets in acting out his message and explaining the purpose of his ministry. The story of Zacchaeus is included in this book because it is a real life account of the parable of the Lost Sheep. It also illustrates graphically that great statement in Luke's gospel, "The Son of Man came to seek and to save what was lost." Luke tells us that Jesus said these words in the midst of his encounter with Zacchaeus. Unfortunately, the story of Zacchaeus has been relegated to the Sunday school class. But it really does not belong there, because as we shall see, it gives us some insight into the meaning of the cross.

This true-life story takes place in the last week of Jesus' life on earth. A man who knows he has only seven days to live can be forgiven if he indulges in thinking about himself. He needs some privacy, some time alone to think and prepare for the horrible death awaiting him. Yet in the midst of a hectic week which was full of emotion and pain, Jesus finds the time to heal a poor blind man and to talk at length with the notorious chief tax collector, Zacchaeus.

Jesus' schedule for that week was frenetic. On Saturday, he stayed in Jericho. The next day, he rides triumphantly into Jerusalem. His activities in Jerusalem that week included going into the temple and clearing out the traders and entering into disputations with the religious authorities. The last two days was spent with his disciples including sharing with them the Passover. He was arrested, endured the mockery of a trial at night and crucified the next day.

What a week it was! A week that changed the world.

As he approached Jericho, Jesus was met by a large crowd. The Middle Eastern way of greeting the arrival of someone important was to send a delegation of dignitaries outside the town or village to meet the visitor before they entered it. The more important the visitor the further out the welcoming party went. So it is here in this scene. The important men of the city were already there to escort him into Jericho. This explains why by the time blind Bartimaeus met Jesus there was already a crowd around him.

This still happens today in the East. When I was a boy my hero was Lee Kuan Yew, who later became the first Prime Minister of Singapore. When he visited our little village in Malaysia, his cavalcade was met at the edge of the community. He got out of his car and walked in procession with the local village leaders into the village. This is the same picture we have of the *parousia*, for when Jesus returns, we will "go out" to meet him in the air to welcome him back.

There is a buzz of excitement in the crowd milling around Jesus. They know he is on his way to Jerusalem. They have heard about what he has done, the miracles, his teaching. They have seen him cast out demons. So they wonder what is going to happen next. Will he lead a popular uprising when he gets to Jerusalem, overthrow the hated Romans and restore Israel to its former glory? They were busy talking and excited, so when Bartimaeus starts shouting, "Jesus, Son of David, have mercy on me!" they told him, "Be quiet! He's too busy!" This crowd is anticipating great things as Jesus heads towards Jerusalem and here is this blind man trying to attract his attention! "Not today, Bartimaeus, not today!"

But Bartimaeus is determined to overcome all obstacles to meet Jesus. It shows the hunger he had in his heart. How desperate are we that God should hear us? Do we easily get put off by obstacles and give up? Bartimaeus could have given up because of the people around and because Jesus had more important things to do than spend time with him. Instead he shouts even louder for the Master's attention.

Jesus stops and has this blind man brought to him. He then asks Bartimaeus a seemingly strange question: "What do you want me to do for you?" It is like Jesus, with his power of healing, walking into a hospital ward and asking the patients a similar question. It may be obvious, but it is always good for us to articulate what is on our heart. Jesus knew full well what this man wanted. Bartimaeus answered: "Lord, I want to see." The Syriac version of the Bible adds a wonderful extra bit to this reply: "I want to receive my sight in order that I might see you."

Jesus heals Bartimaeus because of his faith. When the crowd saw that this blind man could now see, the excitement rose even more. They knew he had been blind from birth. As soon as he could see, Bartimaeus began following Jesus. He was praising God and all the people who saw this praised God, too.

The crowd witnessed this miraculous healing at Jericho knowing that Jesus was on his way to Jerusalem and that something great and momentous was expected to happen there. They would have been aware that only the Messiah was capable of performing this miracle and their expectations would have soared. When Jesus began his earthly ministry, he said: "The Spirit of the Lord is upon me because He has anointed me to proclaim good news to the poor and recovery of sight to the blind ..." (Lk. 4). This miracle was a Messianic act. As if a match has been lit, the crowd now goes wild with excitement. They think they are on to something really momentous.

Jesus had intended to pass through Jericho. By the time he met Zacchaeus, Jesus had already decided to spend the night in Jerusalem, not in Jericho. Verse 1 of chapter 19 tells us that - he was already on his way out of town. We also know that he was passing through Jericho from the details supplied by Luke about the sycamore tree.

The sycamore is an interesting tree. It is short with a thick trunk. The wood was used to build houses. It was an easy tree to climb into. The big leaves made it good for hiding in. Figs sprouted from the trunks, but because of their low sugar content only the poor would eat them. Most of the time they dropped to the ground and were left to rot. Birds were attracted to the tree, making an even bigger mess. So the rabbis ordered that all sycamores should be planted at least eighty feet outside the town boundary.

So we know that Jesus was now outside the town, having turned down the invitations to spend the night in Jericho. When an important person comes to town in the Middle or Far East, it would be a great honour to persuade him to stay at your house. All the important people in the town or village would fight for the privilege of being the host to the visitor. What this story tells us is that Jesus had already turned down the invitations of these important men of Jericho to spend the night there. It is important to see that he had planned to go straight to Jerusalem when he encountered Zacchaeus on the way.

Jericho was seventeen miles from Jerusalem and could be walked in several hours. The road was dangerous, as we have seen from the parable of the Good Samaritan. This was the place to get mugged, but Jesus was not afraid because he had his disciples and the crowd with him. Just outside Jericho, Jesus comes across Zacchaeus up a tree.

Scene 1: Zacchaeus and his wealth
Every Jewish boy has to decide at some point whether to become a *haborim*, which means a "companion or learned one" with a trade, spending his spare time studying the Law, or to become an *am-har-rets*, a "son of the land." These two groups hate each other's guts. This is why there were certain categories of trade in the New Testament which are really despised. You were a sinner if you simply belonged to one of these despised professions.

Shepherds, for example, were outcasts. They did not wash

their hands before they ate and did not keep the Law. They let their animals feed in other people's fields and could not be trusted when they sold wool and milk because you did not know whether it was theirs or somebody else's. They were not allowed into the synagogues. They were *am-har-rets*. Interestingly, teachers of children, butchers and doctors were also despised professionals, the latter because their medicine did not heal anyone, as the account of the woman who had a haemorrhage for twelve years and spent all her money on doctors emphasises.

But the most despised trade of all was that of the tax collector. They were regarded as gutter level - bottom of the pile. They were ostracised and barred from the synagogue. And Zacchaeus was one of them. However, he was no ordinary tax collector. He was the chief tax collector and he had become very rich. Margaret Thatcher, when she was Prime Minister, thought she was on to something new when she advocated large-scale privatisation. But she obviously had not read her Bible because privatisation of tax collection was already in the Scriptures! In Roman times, the area governor decided on the amount of money that needed to be collected from Jericho and would then open up the contract for tender. Whoever put in the best bid (helped, of course, by political connections) won the contract. He would then hire an army of tax collectors and send them out to collect the money for him.

The junior tax collectors did all the dirty work while Zacchaeus simply sat and grew wealthy. He would count all the money brought to him, take his large cut and give the rest to the Roman governor. The system worked very well. Jericho was an excellent place for a tax collecting career, for all the trade between Jerusalem and Jordan had to pass through this city. All Zacchaeus had to do was sit at the bridge and count the money.

Zacchaeus is seen to have become rich through unjust methods. That is why Luke makes the point that he "was wealthy" (19:2). He grew rich on extortion. He abused the power given to him by his Roman employers to line his own pockets. Furthermore, in the time of Jesus, tax collectors were collaborators with the Romans and were therefore doubly hated. During the Second

World War, French collaborators who worked with the Germans against their own people were similarly hated. Zacchaeus was a Roman collaborator, a traitor, despised, treated as an outcast and deeply hated. It is ironic that his name, *Zakkai*, means "Innocent!"

Scene 2: The crowd's excitability

Zacchaeus may have been Mr Big as far as collecting taxes was concerned, but he was a little man physically. His lack of height prevented him from seeing Jesus from the middle of a highly excitable crowd. That such an important and influential man in the city was hemmed in shows the people's hostility towards him. He was simply being ignored by the crowd. Normally, an important person would have been shown courtesy by the crowd parting to let him come to the front to greet the respected visitor. That this did not occur shows the antagonism of the crowd towards Zacchaeus.

Like Bartimaeus though, Zacchaeus was not put off by the problem of the crowd. He now does two unusual things - he runs and he climbs a tree. To someone in the Middle East, these two actions were shocking.

It was both unusual and disgraceful for an important Middle Eastern man to run in public. Slaves and servants can run, but not important old men. Such men wore long, flowing robes, making it difficult to move quickly. To run they had to bend down and pull up the hem of their robes up to the middle of their thighs, exposing their underwear! The rich, as we have seen in the Rich Man and Lazarus, wore expensive purple robes and designer linen underwear. Important men in the Middle and Far East just do not run anywhere. Everybody else can wait for them. A man's importance could be seen by the manner of his walk. The slower he walked the more important he was. As we have noted, the only other person we see running in the Bible is the father of the Prodigal son. Yet Zacchaeus wanted to see Jesus so much that he was willing to disgrace himself publicly by running. It showed the bankruptcy in his heart despite all his wealth. Nothing was going to stop him seeing Jesus.

Having ran, Zacchaeus then climbed a tree. When did you last see a mayor climbing a tree? Important people do not do such outlandish things, certainly not in the Middle East. It is not very dignified and in the East cheeky little boys have a habit of taking a peep at the underwear of a person who does so! That was what my friends and I did as youngsters when sarong-clad men climbed trees to pick mangoes or coconuts. Villages anywhere were littered with such little boys. That was why it was shameful to climb trees in public.

But Zacchaeus emphasises his desperation to see Jesus by being willing to be publicly humiliated in this way. Like Bartimaeus, he did not mind making a spectacle of himself. He had heard about Jesus by reputation. Now he wanted to see him. There was no point asking for an appointment. It was likely to be refused in view of his own reputation.

Scene 3: Jesus' offer of unexpected love

Imagine the scene. There is the very excited crowd following their champion on the way to Jerusalem. Suddenly Jesus stops, seeing the man they hate so much, literally up a tree. When Jesus fixes his eyes on Zacchaeus, so do a few hundred other pairs of eyes. Some of the onlookers are rubbing their hands, thinking: "Good! We've got him now!" They wanted his blood - and they thought that they were about to get it. If looks could kill, Zacchaeus would have been dead from the gazes of the crowd.

Zacchaeus, feeling extremely vulnerable up this tree, is expecting the most severe telling-off of his life, for he knows he is not the most popular man in town. The crowd is expecting Jesus to be tough with him. They would have felt justice was done if Jesus would preach a strong sermon along these lines: "Zacchaeus, you are a sinner and a traitor! You've exploited your fellow countrymen without a shred of mercy or compassion. The judgement of God is upon you ..." If Jesus had said something like that the crowd would have applauded him.

But he does not. Instead, Jesus does the unexpected and says: "Zacchaeus, come down immediately. I must stay at your house today." It was the most unexpected offer of divine love and totally undeserved. Here Jesus is trying to teach us that this is the kind of love that the Father has for each one of us. Zacchaeus deserves judgement, condemnation, anger and hostility. Instead Jesus makes him this generous offer. Having already turned down the invitations from all Jericho's important men to stay with them, he changes his programme to spend the night in the home of a sinner! In an age of spin doctors and political advisers, this would be considered a bad decision by Jesus. The publicity the next day would be calamitous.

So Zacchaeus immediately climbs down from the tree and welcomes Jesus gladly, literally with "rejoicing." This word "joy" is one we have encountered several times in the other parables. In the Lost Sheep and the Lost Coin there is rejoicing in the presence of the angels over one sinner who repents. When Zacchaeus, this sinner and outcast, is received into the friendship and love of God there is rejoicing in heaven - and in Zacchaeus's heart as well. The sheep could never have rejoiced, although it was no doubt glad to see the shepherd, and the coin could never rejoice, but Zacchaeus, this lost sheep of Israel, could rejoice and did so. He has been found by the shepherd, Jesus, and brought home. And there is great rejoicing. This is a real life version of the parable of the Lost Sheep.

Scene 4: The crowd's hostility

The crowd was astonished, disappointed and angry when they saw this. They started "murmuring among themselves." Up till then they had been very happy and excited, all championing Jesus. Even when they saw Zacchaeus up the tree they were in good humour, urging the Master, "Go for him, Jesus! Go for him!" But when Jesus announced that he wanted to spend the night in the hated tax collector's house, the mood suddenly changed.

"He has gone to be the guest of a sinner," they complained. The Jewish religious leaders taught that there were a number of ways a person could become defiled by sin. One way was to sit on the seat of a sinner, so if a tax collector sat there and you sat on the same spot after he had left, you would be contaminated. Another was to sit at a sinner's table. People ate from a communal dish by dipping pieces of bread into it. Jesus took a lot of stick because he often ate with sinners. A third way to become defiled was to sleep on a sinner's bed. Jesus, the crowd and Zacchaeus knew that if Jesus spent the night at the tax collector's house, he would be ceremonially unclean the next morning.

On his way to his death on the cross then, Jesus was willing to identify himself with a sinner. He was willing to become defiled by Zacchaeus' sin, to take the hostility that the tax collector deserved, upon himself. By doing so Jesus became the villain instead of the hero - for the crowd's hostility towards Zacchaeus was now directed at him. It is almost as if Jesus was saying prophetically to the people around him: "If you want to understand the meaning of the cross then understand what I'm doing here with Zacchaeus." Here then is the shadow of the cross in the story for Jesus took upon himself our sins. He was defiled and became sin for our sakes. God's judgement was transferred to him like the scapegoat in Leviticus, where once a year the sins of the nation would be transferred to the animal and it would be led away to the wilderness to take away those sins. Some of the deepest meanings of the cross are here. This is why this story should not be relegated to the Sunday school.

In his dealings with Zacchaeus, the Lord already felt something of the deepest agonies of the Cross. He knew what was going to happen in a week's time. It was bad enough for the crowd to turn against him and say awful things about him at Jericho, but Calvary would be far, far worse.

Scene 5: Zacchaeus and his wealth
Zacchaeus shows real faith and repentance: "Look, Lord! Here and now I give half of my possessions to the poor, and if I have cheated anybody out of anything, I will pay back four times the amount." The story returns to Zacchaeus' wealth. Giving half of it away does not mean he would live the rest of his life in poverty, but it did mean that he was no longer a prisoner to material riches.

Just as he did two unusual things to see Jesus, Zacchaeus now shows his repentance in two unusual ways. First of all he calls Jesus "Lord ..." He has changed his allegiance from his Roman masters to Jesus. Secondly, he demonstrates his generosity by offering to give away half of what he owns and to repay those he had defrauded. This is incredible. Jesus had not even preached a sermon to him about tithing or stewardship! He did not need to. Zacchaeus demonstrated that he had been genuinely touched by the grace of God by responding generously. When a person confessed to fraud and makes voluntary restitution, the Law required him to return the amount stolen plus twenty per cent (Lev. 5:1-5; Num. 5:5-7). If a thief was caught in the act he must pay back double (Ex. 22:7). But a man stealing what is essential was required to pay back fourfold (Ex. 22:1; 2 Sam. 12:6). Zacchaeus, fully repentant, voluntarily imposed on himself the full restitution required by the Law. This was a remarkable act. He had gone beyond the requirements of the Law because he had experienced the extravagant love of God.

Jesus then pronounces this man as a person who is saved: "Today salvation has come to this house because this man, too, is a son of Abraham." In other words, Zacchaeus has been an outcast for so long, but now he is being restored to his own people. Scholars have noticed an interesting play on words here. The Hebrew word for salvation is *yeshu'ah* and Jesus' name in Hebrew is *Yeshua*. *Yeshua*/salvation has literally "come to this house." That is one of the things God does to us when he saves us; he brings us into his family. Those who have been touched by God's love discover new brothers and friends in his family.

Jesus finishes with this great mission statement: "The Son of Man has come to seek and to save what was lost." You can preach a sermon on that verse alone, but you could not do any better than to tell the story of Zacchaeus. It fills out the meaning of this great mission statement. Jesus was busy that day yet he found time for an insignificant sinner like Bartimaeus. Then he found time again for a hated, greedy man, Zacchaeus, because it is in the heart of God to seek and save the lost. He will stop at nothing to do so. He is never too busy.

What happened to Zacchaeus is very exciting. He was touched by the spirit of jubilee. The jubilee was an economic programme that God instituted in Old Testament times. It meant that there would be a re-distribution of wealth every fiftieth year. All debts and mortgage loans would be cancelled, all slaves freed, everyone would have a year's holiday so that the land, animals and servants had rest. Homes were to be returned to their original owners.

It was so radical that the Jews never practised it! But Jesus began his earthly ministry with the jubilee words from Isaiah 61: "The Spirit of the Lord is upon me, because he has anointed me to bring good news to the poor ... and to proclaim the year of the Lord's favour." That was the jubilee year. What had been neglected and forgotten in Old Testament times had been taken up by Jesus and interpreted in an even more radical way. Where the jubilee was supposed to happen once every half-century, it is now to take place every day! The jubilee spirit is about justice, rediscovering family, of being generous to each other. The crowd had understood the significance of Bartimaeus' healing. It was a Messianic act. However, they failed to understand that Zacchaeus' offer of jubilee distribution was also a result of a Messianic act. When Messiah comes he will introduce jubilee. We see it here with Zacchaeus. We see it again on the day of Pentecost where the disciples shared what they had with everyone who had need.

I spent eight years living in such a community, sharing our goods, possessions and nearly everything else. We practised generosity towards each other. It was hard, costly and sacrificial, but they were great years. And Zacchaeus was touched with something of that spirit. The generosity of God affected him and opened his tight-fisted mind. Imagine a Jew giving away half his wealth and repaying those he had cheated fourfold. That is real repentance!

This is then the real life version of the parable of the lost sheep which the Shepherd has found and brought home to great rejoicing. It is a demonstration of the extraordinary generosity of God. Couched in this marvellous story, however, we find Jesus revealing to us the meaning of the Cross.

We began our study with the parable of the Two Debtors and saw the prodigal daughter restored to fellowship with God. It is appropriate that we end with the story of Zacchaeus, a prodigal son, a lost sheep who is also restored to a relationship with God.

APPENDIX

SUMMARY OF THE PARABLES

Scholars see the parable of Jesus as describing various aspects of the Kingdom of God. It may be helpful to readers to see the parables classified into seven groups stating different aspects about the Kingdom of God.

1. The Kingdom has come

There are parables that seek to tell us that the Kingdom of God has come among men. In some measure the Kingdom has invaded Planet Earth. One of the parables that come under this category is about the Bridegroom and his guests. Do people fast at a wedding? Jesus asked. No. They celebrate and rejoice. That is what happens when the Bridegroom is among the people. Jesus is trying to tell us in this group of parables that the Kingdom of Heaven has broken in and invaded the kingdom of men and the Bridegroom, the King, is in the midst. He is going away, and coming back, but he is here among us now.

Examples: Bridegroom's guest, New wine, Strong man, Unshrunk cloth.

2. The Kingdom is still to come

This group of parables tell us that whilst in one sense the kingdom is among us, nevertheless the fullness of the kingdom is still to come. And their message is: "Don't be contented. There are bigger things to come." The parable about the Talents seeks to tell us that, so does the one about the thief coming in the night and the one about the Wise and Foolish Virgins. On the one hand, the Kingdom is among us and we can rejoice and have freedom, while on the other, the fullness of the Kingdom is in the future. So the parables tell us to be faithful, patient and watchful. They also tell us that there will be a judgement to come.

Examples: Wise and Foolish Virgins, Budding of the fig tree, the Thief, the Talents.

3. The Kingdom belongs to the poor and lost

This is probably the best-known group of stories and includes most peoples' favourites. There's the Lost Sheep, the Lost Coin and especially the Lost Sons, where the elder son as well as the Prodigal son was lost. In this parable, Jesus is saying that there are two ways of being lost. One is lost away from home and the other lost at home, meaning that religion or even sitting in church week by week will not save a person. One of the great statements of the gospel of Luke is, "The Son of Man came to seek and to save what was lost" (Luke 19:10). This is why Jesus spent so much time eating with sinners and among the prostitutes and outcasts, because he is saying they are the ones who are lost. The Kingdom belongs to the likes of these. In these parables, we see Jesus talking about grace for those who do not deserve mercy and forgiveness.

Examples: Lost Sheep, Lost Coin, Lost Sons, Pharisee and Tax Collector, Labourers in the Vineyard.

4. The Kingdom is growing

This group of stories tells us that the Kingdom is not static, but is growing all the time. The parable of the Sower tell us that the Kingdom of God is like a seed that has been planted and grows slowly. We should not expect everything to come by sudden outpourings of the Spirit, as exciting as that might be. We have witnessed the tremendous growth of the church in the Far East, South America and Africa. The church is the fastest growing organisation in the world. It is growing faster now than at any time in its history. Every day some 40,000 new members are added to the church. That is how fast the Church is growing now. Jesus' parables seek to tell us that this growth is sometimes unseen - it is in the soil, but it is growing.

Examples: The Sower, Mustard seed, Yeast, the Net.

5. The Kingdom is very demanding

There's the parable about the Pearl of Great Price. What do you do when you find such a pearl? You have to make a decision. Jesus uses these parables to emphasise that a decision is needed when we are confronted with the Kingdom. It is demanding - of our all. There are the parables of the Rich Fool and the Rich Man and Lazarus. Jesus talks about doors - narrow ones and wide ones - and roads. We have to choose. Jesus uses these parables to draw out a decision from the disciples.

Examples: Hidden Treasure and Pearl, Roads and doors, Rich Fool, Rich Man and Lazarus.

6. The Kingdom is revolutionary

In the Good Samaritan, Jesus is saying that those who have been touched by the love of God need to be revolutionary in the way they relate to each other across racial barriers. The Unmerciful Servant is also a story Jesus uses to emphasise the revolutionary relationships that will be seen among Kingdom people. At the heart of these relationships is mercy. Because God has been merciful towards me, I must be merciful towards others. The unmerciful servant was forgiven so much, but because someone else couldn't afford to repay him a small debt, he ruthlessly had him thrown into prison.

Examples: Good Samaritan, Unmerciful Servant, Unjust Steward.

7. The Kingdom is powered by prayer

The last group of parables tell of the power behind the Kingdom: prayer. There is the story of the Friend at Midnight, about knocking on somebody's door at a distinctly unsociable hour and asking for help to feed an unexpected visitor. The story tells us that the God who answers our prayers is a generous heavenly Father who will give us more than we can ever ask. We can therefore pray with confidence. The other parable in this section is the unjust judge and the widow. The woman kept pestering the judge until he gave in to her request for justice. In telling this lovely story, Jesus brings home to us that the real power behind the Kingdom is persistent prayer, to learn how to keep asking.

Examples: Friend at Midnight, Unjust Judge.

BIBLIOGRAPHY

K Bailey, *Poet and Peasant and Through Peasant Eyes* (Eerdmans)

C Blomberg, *Interpreting the Parables* (IVP)

A Edersheim, *The Life and Times of Jesus the Messiah* (Longmans & Co)

AM Hunter, *Interpreting the Parables* (SCM)

J Jeremias, *Jerusalem in the Times of Jesus* (SCM)

J Jeremias, *The Parables of Jesus* (SCM)

IH Marshall, *The Gospel of Luke* (NIGTC, Paternoster)

DH Stern, *Jewish New Testament Commentary* (JNT Publications)

H Thielicke, *The Waiting Father: Sermons on the Parables of Jesus* (James Clarke)

JA Thompson, *Handbook of Life in Bible Times* (IVP)

D Wenham, *The Parables of Jesus* (Hodder & Stoughton)

63714730R00088

Made in the USA
Charleston, SC
11 November 2016